# Irish Baby Names

# Irish Baby Names

Mairéad Byrne

## foulsham

LONDON • NEW YORK • TORONTO • SYDNEY

# foulsham

Capital Point, 33 Bath Road, Slough, Berkshire SL1 3UF,
England

Foulsham books can be found in all good bookshops or direct
from www.foulsham.com

ISBN: 978-0-572-04749-8

Cover photograph © Superstock

A CIP record for this book is available from the British Library

Printed in Great Britain by Martins the Printers, Berwick upon Tweed

# Contents

# Introduction

The Irish have always been great travellers, so their names, like the people, have spread throughout the world. Today, Irish names – as all things Irish – are enjoying enormous popularity.

This book offers you a choice of 300 Irish names for your new baby: 150 each for boys and girls. You'll find the most popular current choices (in 2005 the top five for girls were Siobhan, Aisling, Deirdre, Niamh and Eileen, and for boys, Aidan, Liam, Declan, Ciarán and Conor), along with lots of very old names and many unusual ones.

In Ireland, many names are used for both sexes, with surnames often used as first names too.

Far more Irish boys' names exist than girls', reflecting the fact that Ireland was a patriarchal society, and most historical records are concerned with the activities of men not women.

## Making your choice

Many Irish names have several different spellings, which have been moulded and adapted by history. To make it as easy as possible to choose, we have listed girls' and boys' names in alphabetical order, under the most commonly used form of the name, with information on the meaning and background of each.

Where applicable, we've also given alternative spellings, including the Gaelic form if it's different, other older forms and the anglicised version if there is one. In some cases, the anglicised spelling is now the most commonly used form.

So you'll often find that not only do you have a choice of name, but a choice of the form too. You may prefer the spelling and sound of an older version of a name to the contemporary one. You're spoiled for choice!

# Where do Irish names come from?

Irish names reflect the country's turbulent history. Over 12,000 Irish names were recorded in early sources, with thousands falling out of use in the Middle Ages. Many were introduced into Ireland by invaders, with the Irish adopting the names and finding their own forms.

Some have Celtic origins: the Celts – or Gaels – arrived from about 700 BC onwards, bringing the Gaelic language to Ireland. Other names came in with the Norse invaders – the Vikings – in the ninth and tenth centuries.

Christianity, which was brought to Ireland by St Patrick in the fifth century, is also a source: names with Christian and Hebrew origins remain popular. Others are drawn from Latin, Greek and the Teutonic languages.

Many are saints' names. The Irish have hundreds of saints, and some children are given the name of the saint on whose feast day they're born or baptised. Others are the names of Irish heroes or historical figures.

Most names, however, came from the French and then the English invaders (the Anglo-Normans) from the twelfth to the fourteenth century; many of the English names had Saxon and Germanic origins. These Anglo-Norman names almost entirely supplanted the old Gaelic ones.

The process continued under the Tudor and Stuart settlements and under Cromwellian rule and colonisation in the seventeenth century. As English became the dominant language, particularly in the nineteenth century, English, biblical and classical names replaced indigenous Irish ones.

However, the Gaelic revival, in the late nineteenth and early twentieth centuries, saw a return to fashion of many old names drawn from Gaelic myths, legends and folklore.

Some names are so well travelled (e.g. Brian, Sheila) that the original Irish source of the name has almost been forgotten. Others have become so international (e.g. Kevin) that the modern anglicised spelling has taken on a life of its own, apart from its original Gaelic form (Caoimhín).

The influence of mass media (television, radio and the internet), along with cheap travel and mass tourism, are also factors. The world gets ever smaller, with Irish names exported worldwide and new names from other parts of the world added to the 'Irish collection' all the time. The popularity of some of these new names may endure; others may vanish as quickly as they arrived – in some cases, mercifully.

# Why choose an Irish name?

Many factors influence parents in their choice of name. They may want to continue a family tradition, by giving a child a relative's name, often a grandparent, or one traditionally used in their family.

Those with an Irish background may choose a name that reflects their heritage: their patriotism for Ireland and its history.

Parents' own religion may be a factor: some names are specific to Catholic families, and Catholics often name their children after a pope.

There's also a current revival of interest in old Irish names, in names of historical figures who became saints and in names from Celtic mythology. You may find yourself so beguiled by the stories from Celtic myth and legend that you want to find out more. Plenty of websites carry information on the most famous Irish epic stories; www.babynamesof ireland.com is one of the best.

Fashion and changes in taste are also deciding factors. The current popularity of Irish names is just one manifestation of the vogue for all things Irish over the last 15 years or so, from theatre to tourism. The Celtic economic tiger is still roaring. Since the late 1980s it has changed Ireland – and the attitudes of the rest of the world to Ireland – out of all recognition.

The rich and expressive meanings of Irish names also account for their popularity. You can, if you wish, name your child according to the colour of their hair or their skin (dark, fair or red, for example); after flowers, trees, animals or birds; or after their individual qualities. Whatever your baby's looks or character, you'll find a name to fit.

Finally, the attractive nature of an Irish name is often reason enough to choose it. Whether you have Irish connections or not, the older forms, including the Gaelic, have poetry in them: they sound and look just beautiful.

*Please note:*

1. In the information provided with each name the form *mac Néill* means 'son of Niall'; *Mac Neill* is the Irish surname; *MacNeill* is the anglicised surname.
2. All dates are AD, unless stated otherwise.

# Irish Gaelic

Gaelic is a Celtic language, part of the Indo-European family of languages. There are several types: Irish Gaelic, Scottish Gaelic, and Manx form one group; Welsh, Cornish and Breton another. Irish Gaelic is usually just referred to as Irish, and we have followed this convention here.

Until the seventeenth century, Irish Gaelic (pronounced 'Gallic') was spoken by the whole Irish population. By the nineteenth century, the dominance of English had almost made it extinct. There was a Gaelic revival at the end of the nineteenth century and the beginning of the twentieth, however, and again after the formation of the Irish Free State in the south in 1922. A standard written form of Irish Gaelic was instituted in 1945.

Today about 500,000 people speak Irish, about one-seventh of the population of the Republic of Ireland. Irish Gaelic is the official language, but English has become the primary spoken language. However, the government has set up revival programmes for Irish Gaelic and it is now taught in all Irish schools.

The Irish alphabet has only 18 letters (13 consonants and 5 vowels), compared to 26 in English. The remaining letters appear in words that have been borrowed from other languages, but are not used in Irish Gaelic words.

Some Irish words resemble English ones, but have a very different meaning: *bean* means 'woman', *fear* means 'man', *bád* means 'boat'. Unlike English words, Irish words also have a gender, as in French or Italian, but it is not always logical: *cailín* ('girl') is masculine and *bean* ('woman') is feminine.

# Spelling and pronunciation

Many Irish names have so many different spellings (they were recorded in Latin, French or English as well as Irish) that it's impossible to be definitive. Just choose the spelling you prefer.

Similarly, pronunciation of the Irish form of names is a minefield for non-Gaelic speakers. Words are not pronounced phonetically and there are many differences in dialect.

There are three main dialects in the south of Ireland: Munster (Cork and Kerry), Connacht (Connemara) and Ulster (Donegal). Within these there are also many local differences, giving varied pronunciation even for names as common as Sean and Deirdre, so it's impossible to give definitive guidance. The best advice is to ask a good local speaker of Irish.

The short pronunciation guide below will give you some general rules, however, though there are many exceptions to the rules.

## Pronunciation guide
*Vowels*

Irish vowels are either long or short. Long vowels are marked with an acute accent, called a *fada* in Irish, which means 'long'.

In Irish names the stress is strong and usually falls on the first syllable. Vowels in later syllables are pronounced very lightly, unless they are accented and therefore pronounced long.

*Short vowels (no accent)*

Pronounce these as:

| | |
|---|---|
| a | as English O as in *pot* |
| e | as English E as in *pet* (except when it comes before A, when it is silent) |
| i | as English I as in *pit* (some exceptions) |
| o | as English U as in *smut* |
| u | as English U as in *pull* |

*Long vowels (with accent)*

Pronounce these as:

| | |
|---|---|
| á | as English AW as in *call* (e.g. Siobhán) |
| é | as English AY as in *came* |
| í | as English EE as in *see* |

| ó | as English O as in *sow* |
| ú | as English OO as in *too* |

*Vowel combinations*
Pronounce these as:

| ei | as English I as in *vine* |
| ow | as English OW as in *owl* |

*Consonants*
Irish Gaelic has only 13 consonants (B, C, D, F, G, H, L, M, N, P, R, S, T), fewer than English, and most are pronounced very much like English.

Consonants are either palatal, pronounced by raising the front of the tongue towards the hard palate (the roof of the mouth), or non-palatal, so pronounce:

| c and g | always hard (as English *came* and *game*) |
| s | as SH before e or i (e.g. *Sean*: pronounced Shawn) |
| sh | as H |
| th | as H |
| bh, mh | as V (sometimes as W) |
| dh, fh and gh | usually silent (e.g. *Laoghaire*: pronounced Leary) |
| ch | as guttural K (e.g. Scottish *loch*) |

*Broad and slender*
Irish vowels can either be broad (a, o, u and á, ó, ú) or slender (e, i and é, í).

Irish consonants are also broad or slender. Broad consonants are preceded or followed by a broad vowel (a, o, u or á, ó ú) and are non-palatal. Slender consonants are preceded or followed by a slender vowel (e, i or é, í) and are palatal.

# Girls' names A to Z

Alternative spelling(s)    Name    Anglicised form(s)

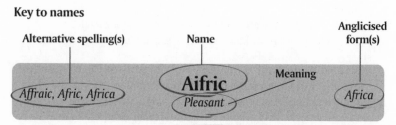

*Affraic, Afric, Africa*    **Aifric**    Meaning    *Africa*

*Pleasant*

The name of two eighth- and ninth-century abbesses of Kildare, who died in 738 and 833 respectively. This may be a Gaelic name, taken from the word for 'pleasant', or it may come from the name of the continent. One namesake was the daughter of Godred, king of the Isle of Man, and wife of John de Courcy. She founded the Cistercian Grey Abbey in the Ards, Co. Down.

Description

# Abaigeal
### Father of joy, joyfulness
*Abigail*

The name of the wife of the biblical King David, who was renowned for her prudence and beauty. It was a very common name in Ireland in the nineteenth century, particularly in the form Abaigh. In the south it was used as a genteel form of the Irish name Gobnait.

*Aibrean*

# Aibreann
### April

*Aibreann* is the word for April in the Irish language, so it would be a perfect name for a baby girl born in that month.

*Affraic, Afric, Africa*

# Aifric
### Pleasant
*Africa*

The name of two eighth- and ninth-century abbesses of Kildare, who died in 738 and 833 respectively. This may be a Gaelic name, taken from the word for 'pleasant', or it may come from the name of the continent. One namesake was the daughter of Godred, king of the Isle of Man, and wife of John de Courcy. She founded the Cistercian Grey Abbey in the Ards, Co. Down.

*Ailbe*

# Ailbhe
### White, fair
*Olive*

A famous bearer of the name was Ailbhe Grúadbrecc, which means 'freckled cheeks'. She was the daughter of Cormac mac Airt. Cailte, a warrior of the Fianna, a warrior band of about 150 chieftains and 4,000 warriors, musicians, poets, priests and physicians, claimed she was 'one of the four best women of her time that ever lay with a man'. She became the mistress of Fionn mac Cumhail, founder and leader of the Fianna, and Ireland's most important mythological hero, when she answered a series of riddles correctly.

13

# Ailis

*Ailís, Alish*     *Noble, well-born*     *Alice, Alicia*

A name introduced into Ireland by the Normans in the French form Aliz; the Irish found their own form. It was the name of a notorious fourteenth-century witch from Kilkenny. Alice the Beautiful, a contemporary of King Arthur, had her face covered by a veil so people would not die at the sight of her beauty.

# Áine

*Radiance, splendour, brilliance*     *Enya*

Áine was the goddess of love and fertility and the daughter of the foster son of the sea god Lir. The kings of Munster claimed her as an ancestor, as did the later Norman family, the FitzGeralds. In the Finn tales, she is one of the wives of Fionn mac Cumhail, Ireland's great mythological hero. Her name occurs in folklore all over Ireland: in Teelin, Co. Donegal, a hill called Cnoc Áine was associated with a mysterious piper and was considered dangerous for young girls. The name was once also used as a male name, but is now exclusively female.

# Aingeal

*Messenger*     *Angela*

A name with a biblical connection, it is the Irish form of 'angel' from the Greek *angelos*, meaning 'divine messenger'. An angel was a messenger of God, hence the name.

# Aisling

*Aislinn*     *Vision, dream*     *Ashling*

A name that has been very popular since the nineteenth century. It was used to describe a type of nostalgic poetry, patriotic and romantic, in which Ireland was personified as a beautiful woman, and then became a personal name. Its lovely sound is part of its attraction.

## Alannah
*Alanna, Alana*
Child

A nineteenth-century form of the Gaelic term of endearment, *a leanbh* ('child'), hence its popularity as a first name.

## Alva
*Almha*

In legend, Almha was an Irish goddess, renowned for her strength and prowess. She was one of the Tuatha Dé Danann ('people of Dana'), a mythical tribe of gods said to have been the ancestors of the Irish people. At Almu in Leinster there is a hill and fortress named after her.

## Aodhamair
*Aedammair, Adamair*
Fire

A girl's name derived from the boy's name Áed ('fire'). It was the name of the first woman said to have been 'given the veil' (made a nun) by St Patrick; her father was called Áed. She founded a nunnery at Drom Dubhain, near Clogher, Co. Tyrone (her feast day: 18 January).

## Aoibheall
*Aíbell*
Radiance, spark, fire

The name of one of the old Irish goddesses, which has retained its pagan associations. Some legends say she is a fairy woman who lives in the fairy mound of Craig Liath, near Killaloe, Co. Clare, and that she appeared to the great Irish high king Brian Boru the night before the Battle of Clontarf in 1014. Other legends mention Aíbell, the daughter of the Ulster warrior Celchar mac Uithechair, and Aíbell Grúuadsolus ('Aíbell of the bright cheeks'), the king of Munster's daughter.

## Aoife

*Aife*

*Beautiful, radiant*

*Eva*

A name, probably that of a goddess, which was very common among the heroines of early Irish legends. Aoife was the sister of the female warrior Scathach, who instructed Cúchulainn, the great Ulster warrior, in the martial arts. Aoife fell in love with him and had his son. The child became a warrior and was later killed by his father, who did not know he was his son. Aoife, the daughter of Diarmaid, king of Leinster, married Strongbow, the leader of the Norman invaders.

## Attracta

*Athracht*

A name with obvious attractions that was very popular at the turn of the nineteenth century. It was the name of a sixth-century saint from Sligo. She founded a nunnery at Killaraght, Co. Mayo, a settlement named after her.

## Báirbre
*Strange, savage, uncouth*

Barbara

A name derived from the Greek word for 'strange'. St Barbara was one of the church's early saints. It is said that her father was turned to ashes by a bolt of lightning when he tried to have her put to death for refusing to renounce Christianity. She became the patron saint of artillerymen.

## Béibhinn

*Bébinn, Béfind, Bébhionn*  *Fair woman*  Bevin, Bevan

A popular name in medieval Ireland, it is derived from *bean* ('woman') and *fionn* ('fair'), and may originally have been used to describe Viking women. The mother and daughter of Brian Boru, the great Irish high king who expelled the Norsemen at the Battle of Clontarf in 1014, both had this name. In Irish mythology, the golden-haired giantess Béibhinn fled from her giant husband Aodh Álainn ('the beautiful') and sought sanctuary with Fionn mac Cumhail, leader of the warrior band the Fianna.

## Bernadette

*Bearnairdín*

An imported name, it is the diminutive of the French form of Bernard. It became very popular after the Virgin Mary was said to have appeared to St Bernadette Soubirous in Lourdes in 1858. She was canonised in 1933.

## Bétéide
*Bé Téite*  *Wanton woman*

In legend, Bétéide was one of the Tuatha Dé Danann, the mythical race said to have been the first inhabitants of Ireland. She was the daughter of Flidais.

## Blánaid
*Bláthnáit, Bláthnat, Bláthnaid*
*Little flower*

Blánaid was the wife of Cú Roí, a king of Munster. She fell in love with Cúchulainn, the Ulster warrior and her husband's rival. Cú Roí's fortress was constructed so that no one could find the entrance. Blánaid revealed the secret entrance to Cúchulainn by pouring milk into a stream that flowed through the fortress. Cúchulainn watched where the milk-stained water emerged, entered the fortress and seized it. Cú Roí was killed and Cúchulainn and Blánaid fled. In vengeance, the king's poet seized her and jumped with her to their deaths from the cliff-top of Cenn Bera, on the Beara peninsula on the west coast of Ireland.

## Branna
*Brannagh*
*Raven-black*

An attractive name taken from the Irish word *bran* ('raven'). It is a way of saying 'beauty with hair as dark as a raven', so it is a perfect name for a black-haired baby girl.

## Bree
*Exalted one*

This could be a form of the name Brigid, or a name in its own right that comes from a similar root. The name suggests spirituality (it means 'exalted one'), and is an element in names currently very popular in the United States, such as Breeanne and Breeanna.

## Brianna
*Briana, Bryana, Brianne*
*Noble, virtuous*

Very popular in the United States and Canada, this is a modern female form of the Irish boy's name Brian.

# Brigid

*Bríd, Brighid, Brigit*     *High goddess, strength*     *Bridget*

The name of the greatest of the Irish saints, and of the Celtic goddess of agriculture, healing and poetry. The latter's festival, Imbolc (1 February), marked the beginning of the Celtic spring. St Brigid of Kildare was born *c*.450 and established a great convent there. She died *c*.523. The custom of plaiting 'Brigid's crosses', made of rushes or straw, takes place on her feast day, also 1 February. The name was so often given to Irish girls that 'Biddy' was used to mean any Irish girl. Many who went to America as maids were automatically called 'Biddy'.

# Bronagh

*Brónach*     *Sorrowful*     *Dolores (see separate entry)*

This was a rare early name in Ireland and at one time was used for girls and boys. Brónach was the patron saint of seafarers. St Brónach's well is found in Kilbroney, Co. Down. The saint's crozier is preserved in Dublin's National Museum and her bell in the Catholic church in Rostrevor. Her feast day: 2 April.

*Caireann*

# Cairenn
*Beloved little one*

*Karen, Karin*

A name that may be derived from the Gaelic *cara* ('beloved'), with the diminutive *-in*, so meaning 'beloved little one'. It could also be an Irish form of the Latin name Carina. Cairenn Chasdubh ('Cairenn of the dark curly hair') was the daughter of the king of the Saxons, the mistress of King Eochu and mother of the great warrior Niall of the Nine Hostages. She was therefore the maternal ancestor of Ireland's high kings. She was harshly treated by Eochu's wife, so a poet fostered Niall until he could claim his inheritance. When Niall became king, he treated Cairenn with love and reverence.

*Caitilín*

# Caitlín
*Pure*

*Cathleen, Kathleen
(see separate entry)*

The name is derived from the old French form Cateline, probably referring to Catherine of Alexandria, said to have been martyred in the early years of the fourth century. St Catherine was associated with courage and purity. The name was introduced into Ireland by the French-speaking Anglo-Normans. During a famine, the Countess Cathleen offered her soul to the devil in exchange for food for the starving. God refused to let him keep it. In the eighteenth century, one of the terms used for Ireland was Caitlín ni Houlihan, a nostalgic reference to the time of the old Irish aristocracy.

*Caoilainn, Cáelfind,
Caoilfhionn*

# Caoilfhinn
*Slender and fair*

*Keelin, Kalin*

A name derived from the Gaelic words *caol* ('slender') and *fionn* ('fair'), it was borne by several saints. Of one it was said: 'This pious lady quickly won the esteem and affection of her sister nuns by her exactness to every duty, as also by her sweet temper, gentle, confiding disposition and unaffected piety.' Her feast day: 3 February.

## Caoimhe
*Beauty, grace, gentleness*

*Keeva, Keva*

A beautiful name and that of a virgin saint from Killeavy, Co. Down (feast day: 2 November). The name may come directly from *caoimhe* (meaning 'gentleness', 'beauty', 'grace') or may be a feminine form of the male name Caoimhín.

## Cara

*Caragh, Caera*

*Friend*

*Cara* is the Irish word for 'friend', so no greater recommendation is needed for this name, which may originally have come from Latin. In Italian, *cara* means 'beloved'.

## Carmel
*Garden*

A popular Catholic name in Ireland, it comes from the Hebrew word for 'garden' and is used as a mark of reverence for Our Lady of Mount Carmel. Mount Carmel is a mountain ridge in north-west Israel, which extends from the Samarian hills to the Mediterranean.

## Cas

*Cass*

*Curly-haired*

A name whose derivation is linked to a tribe called the Dal Cais, who lived in Ireland in the early period. It was then a common boy's name and, like so many Irish names, can also be used for a girl. To the modern ear, it now sounds more suitable for a girl. The surname, and now first name, Cassidy *(see page 22)*, comes from the same root.

## Casey
*In the USA:*
*Casie, Kacie, Kacey*
*Vigilant in war*

A girl's name increasing in popularity, particularly in the United States, it is derived from the popular early Irish name Cathasach. It has several contemporary forms in the USA. It can also be used as a boy's name.

## Cassidy
*Curly-haired*

This is another example of an Irish surname now being used as a first name. The Cassidys possessed healing powers and were physicians to the Maguires, chieftains in Co. Fermanagh from *c.*1300 to 1600. As word of their skills spread, the Cassidys were employed by other Irish chieftains, particularly in the north.

## Catriona
*Caitríona, Caitrin*
*Pure*
*Catherine*

The name became popular after the Crusaders brought home stories about Catherine of Alexandria, a legendary and colourful fourth-century martyr. In Ireland, the name became popular through Norman and English influence and by the fifteenth century it was well established among the Irish aristocracy. St Catherine of Siena, in Italy, also popularised the name.

## Ciara
*Ciar*
*Dark, black*
*(in Italian, bright or clear)*
*Kiera, Kira, Kyra*

A name growing in popularity, mainly because of its beautiful sound. St Ciara of Kilkeary, Co. Tipperary, is said to have put out a fire by the power of her prayers. She established two monasteries, the first and most famous at Kilkeary, and died in 679.
Feast days: 5 January and 16 October.

## Cliona

*Clíodhna, Clídna, Cleona*

The name of a goddess of beauty who lived in the Land of Promise and fell in love with a human being, Ciabhán of the Curling Locks. They fled to Glandore, in Co. Cork, but when they landed a great wave came roaring in and drowned Clíodhna. The wave, one of the three great waves of Ireland, is known as 'Clíodhna's Wave'. In legend, a fairy woman has the name. She is one of the Tuatha Dé Danann, the mythical race of gods said to have first inhabited Ireland. They became the underground 'fairy people', whose fairy mounds are still treated with respect by the superstitious. A Cliona was the fairy patroness of the MacCarthys.

## Clodagh

*Clóideach, Clóda*                                                    *Claudia*

The Clóideach is a tributary of the River Suir, in Co. Waterford, and the name became popular after a Marquis of Waterford chose it for one of his daughters.

## Colleen

*Cailín, Colene, Coleen*
*Girl* or *unmarried woman*

This name comes from the Irish *cailín* ('girl') and has become popular all over the world, particularly in the United States. It was used by people of Irish descent there, and in Australia and South Africa. The success of Australian author Colleen McCullough's televised book, *The Thorn Birds*, in the 1980s, increased its popularity.

## Daimhín
*Little deer*

*Damhán, Daimíne*  *Davina, Davin*

A name taken from the Gaelic word *damh* ('deer'). Here, with the diminutive *-ín*, it means 'little deer'. This form has also produced the surnames Davine and Davane.

## Damhnait
*Fawn*

*Damhnat*  *Devnet*

St Damhnait founded a convent, Tydavnet ('Damhnait's House'), in Co. Monaghan in the sixth century. Her crozier, kept in Dublin's National Museum, was used for the testing of oaths. If someone lied, their mouth became twisted, branding them a liar. Her feast day: 13 June. It is also said to be the name of an Irish virgin martyred in Gheel, Belgium, who is now the town's patron saint. Feast day there: 15 May.

## Dana
*Abundance, wealth*

*Danu, Ana, Anu*

Dana is a very old name, and that of the Irish goddess of abundance, described as 'the mother of the gods of Ireland' by tenth-century king, bishop and scholar Cormac mac Cuilennán. She was the goddess of the Tuatha Dé Danann ('people of Dana'), a mythical race said to have been the first to live in Ireland, and gives her name to a pair of breast-shaped mountains in Co. Kerry. There is also a Christian saint of the name, St Ana (feast day: 18 January).

# Darcy

*Darcey, D'Arcy, Darcie*

*Dark-haired*

Both a first name and a surname, the D'Arcy form probably came to
Ireland with the Normans: it had a long history in France and meant
'fortress'. In Ireland its use was strengthened by the similarity to the
Gaelic adjective *dorcha* ('dark', 'dark-haired'): the Irish surname
O Dorchaidhe means 'descendant of the dark one'. It is a name that
is therefore especially suitable for a dark-haired child. It is a
very popular girl's name in the United States today, but was formerly
also used for boys.

# Darina

*Dáiríne, Daireann*

*Fruitful, bountiful*

*Doreen*

Dáiríne  was the younger daughter of Tuathal Teachthmair, the legendary
king of Tara, in Co. Meath; she married Eochaidh, the king of Leinster,
when his first wife, her sister, Fithir, was said to have died. Both women
died of shame when Dáiríne discovered that Fithir was still alive. As a
result, their father went to war with Leinster and exacted tribute
for many years afterwards. One of the earliest references in legend
to Daireann is about a beautiful young woman who fell in love with
Fionn mac Cumhail. She asked to be his only wife for a year, and then
to have half his time.

# Dechtire

*Tenth child*

Dechtire was the sister of Conchobhar, the king of Ulster, and the
mother of Cúchulainn, the great Ulster warrior. The Irish word *deich*
means 'ten', so Dechtire may have been a tenth child. The fairies (*sive*)
captured her and turned her into a bird, but sometimes she became a
woman again, enabling her to conceive Cúchulainn, whose father was
the sun god Lugh.

# Deirdre

*Deirdriú*

*She who chatters*

Deirdre is the most famous woman in Irish mythology, and a source of fascination to poets and writers. The most beautiful woman of her time, she was bethrothed to Conchobhar mac Nessa, king of the Ulstermen, but loved the young warrior Naoise, the eldest of Usna's three sons (Usna was an Ulster chieftain). They ran away to Scotland with Naoise's brothers, but were tricked into returning to Ireland, where Naoise and his brothers were killed. Deirdre threw herself from a chariot, rather than live with Conchobhar. Her story was celebrated by twentieth-century Irish writers W. B. Yeats and John Millington Synge.

# Dervla

*Dearbháil, Derbáil, Deirbhile*

*Daughter of Fál (Ireland)*
or *daughter of a poet*

An ancient Irish name, originally two words, which may mean 'daughter of Fál', a legendary name for Ireland, or 'daughter of a poet'. St Deirbhile founded a convent in Fallmore, Co. Mayo, in the sixth century. Of a fourteenth-century bearer of the name, the daughter of Áedh O'Donnell, it was said: 'There was never born a woman of her tribe who surpassed her in goodness.' The fame of contemporary Irish travel writer Dervla Murphy has also popularised the name.

# Dervorgilla

*Dearbhorgaill, Dervorguilla*

*Daughter of Forgall*

Forgall was a god and this name means 'daughter of Forgall'. In legend, the name belonged to a woman who loved Cúchulainn, Ulster's great warrior. He rejected her, but they settled their differences and became as close as brother and sister. Dervorguilla was also the name of a twelfth-century queen who left her husband for Diarmaid, the king of a neighbouring province. She established a church at Clonmacnoise.

## Doireann
*Doirind, Dáirinn*          *Daughter of Finn*          *Doreen*

An ancient Irish name, which may mean 'daughter of Finn'. In Irish legend, Doirind and her two sisters, the daughters of Midhir Yellow-mane, were given as wives to the sons of the king of Ireland 'since from wives it is that either fortune or misfortune is derived'. Doirind was also the name of the daughter of Bodh Derg, the son of the Dagda (the 'good god'). She wooed Fionn and gave him a magic potion.

## Dolores
*Sorrows*

A popular Catholic first name in Ireland, it is taken from the Spanish title for the Virgin Mary, Maria de los Dolores ('Mary of the Sorrows').

## Donla
*Donnfhlaidh, Dúnlaith, Dunflaith*          *Brown princess*          *Dunla*

A name that has become very popular in recent years. It has a long history of royal usage, but could also mean 'lady of the fortress' (*dun* means 'fortress'). Dúnlaith was the daughter of the Connacht warrior, Regamon. Others with the name were the daughter of Fogartach, who died in 773; the wife of the high king Niall Frassach; and the daughter of Flaithbertach, a cleric and high king of Ireland. He died in 764 and she in 798.

# Ealga
*Noble*

An attractive and unusual name, rarely used now and so ripe for renewed popularity. It is derived from Innis Ealga ('Noble Isle'), a poetic name for Ireland, so there could be no better reason for choosing this name.

# Echna
*Eachna, Echnach*       *Horse, steed*

A name taken from *each* ('horse', 'steed'). In legend, Echna was the daughter of the king of Connacht. She was reputed to be the cleverest and most beautiful woman of her time. 'The manner of this lady was this: she had three perfections; for of the world's wise women she was one, and he whom she should have counselled had as the result both affluence and consideration.' Of her clothes it was said: 'A smock of royal silk she had next to her skin; over that an outer tunic of soft silk and around her a hooded mantle of crimson fastened on her breast with a golden brooch.'

# Eileen
*Eibhlín, Aileen, Aibhilín*       *Sunlight, life*       *Evelyn, Ellen, Helen*

A name introduced to Ireland by the Normans as Avelina, Evelina and Emeline, which soon found an Irish form. It was the name of many aristocratic women in Norman Ireland, including the wife of Walter de Burgo, the Earl of Ulster, and the daughter of the Red Earl of Ulster. The form Eibhlín became very popular: Eibhlín Dubh Ní Chonaill composed the most beautiful of all Irish laments when her husband died. A love song, '*Eibhlín a Ruan*', written by seventeenth-century harpist Cearbha O'Dalaigh to his lover, persuaded her to elope with him on her wedding day. It is still popular at Irish weddings today.

## Eilís

*Eibhlís, Eilish*          *God has sworn* or *God is satisfaction*          *Elizabeth*

The name of the mother of John the Baptist first came into Ireland with the Anglo-Normans in its Spanish form, Isabella. It was a common Irish name in the Middle Ages. Eilís nic Diarmada Rua was described by the famous blind harpist Turlough Ó Carolan (1670–1732) as 'outshining the rose in beauty'. She was probably the granddaughter of his patrons, the McDermott Roes of Ballyfarnon, Co. Roscommon.

## Einín

*Eneen*          *Little bird*

A contemporary name with an obvious appeal, it has already become established as a popular name. It is derived from *éan* ('bird') with the diminutive *-ín*, hence 'little bird'. Endearments in Ireland, as elsewhere, often took the form of birds.

## Eireen

*Ireland* or *peace*

The derivation of this pretty, contemporary name has been attributed to two sources: it could either be a combination of the word for Ireland, Éire, with the Irish diminutive form '*-een*', or it could be an Irish form of the name Irene, meaning 'peace'. Take your pick.

## Eithne

*Ethna*                    Kernel                    *Edna, Ena*

This was the name of the mother of Lugh, god of the sun and of arts and crafts, and was a common name in Irish mythology. Historically, Eithne was the wife of Congalach mac Máelmithidh, a king killed by the Vikings in 955. Eithne of the Tuatha Dé Danann ('people of Dana'), in legend the original inhabitants of Ireland, lost her demon guardian and became a Christian. It was also a popular name for saints and the mothers of saints. Eithne and Fedelma, daughters of King Laoghaire, shared the shortest life of any Irish saints: they were instructed, baptised, ordained and 'sanctified' in one day in 433.

## Emer

*Eimhear, Eimear*

Emer was the daughter of Forgall Manach of Leinster. She was said to possess the 'six gifts of womanhood': beauty, a gentle voice, sweet words, wisdom, chastity – and needlework, and was the wife of the great Ulster warrior Cúchulainn. Her father objected to the match, but Cúchulainn single-handedly stormed his fortress and carried Emer off. She bore Cúchulainn's unfaithfulness until he made love to Fand, wife of the sea god Lir. When Emer confronted them, she realised how much Fand loved him and offered to withdraw. Fand was so touched that she returned to her husband. When Cúchulainn died, Emer spoke lovingly at his graveside.

## Erin

*Erinn, Eryn, Erina*              Of Eire

Erin probably means 'of Eire', and is a form of Éire, the name of the goddess that Ireland was named after. In legend, she was one of the Tuatha Dé Danann ('people of Dana'), the ancient gods and inhabitants of Ireland. It is not surprising, therefore, that this name was so widely used by Irish immigrants to Australia, Canada and the United States.

## Étáin
*Éadaoin, Eadain*

*Jealousy*

*Edwina*

According to Celtic mythology, Étáin was 'the most beautiful woman in all Ireland'. The god Midir fell in love with her and took her home. His jealous wife changed Étáin into a pool of water, a worm and then a fly, to hinder his search for her. The fly was blown about by the wind for twice seven years, until it fell into a glass of wine that was drunk by a woman who wanted a child. She gave birth to a daughter, also called Étáin. After many other travails, Étáin and Midir were reunited. It is also the name of the patron saint of Moylurg (Boyle), Co. Roscommon (feast day: 5 July).

## Fainche
*Fanchea*

*Crow*

*Fanny*

The name of many Irish saints, including St Fanchea of Rossory, Co. Fermanagh, who established a monastery there; her brother was Enda of Aran, the father of Irish monasticism, and she persuaded him to take up the religious life. An early king of Cashel, Óengus mac Natfraich, had been a suitor of hers. She was sure she was destined for the religious life, so she successfully steered him towards her sister Dáiríne. Her feast day: 1 January. Fainche is also the name of the saint of Cluain-caoi, near Cashel. Feast day: 21 January.

# Fallon
*Faithleann, Fallamhan*
## Leader

A contemporary name that is gaining in popularity, it comes from the old Irish names Faithleann or Fallamhan. It is also a surname (with a second form, Falloon), but is now used more and more as a first name, for girls and boys. To modern tastes it seems more appropriate for a girl.

# Fianna
## Warrior

The Fianna were Fionn mac Cumhail's band of warriors. In early Ireland, women had equal rights with men, and though warriors were usually men there is a tradition dating from Roman times of Celtic women fighting alongside men, hence this name for a girl. It could also be a combination of the two names Fiona ('wine') and Anna ('full of grace').

# Fidelma
*Fedelm, Feidhelm*
## Constancy

A traditional Gaelic name at least 1,500 years old and given to many saints and Irish mythological figures, it was also the name of many famous women in ancient Ireland. Fedelm Noícrothach ('the nine times beautiful') was a female warrior and the daughter of Conchobhar mac Nessa, king of Ulster. She was married to Cairpre Nia Fer, by whom she had a son, Erc, but she eloped with the Ulster warrior Conall Cearnach. He was the foster brother and cousin of the great Ulster warrior Cúchulainn and avenged the latter's death.

## Fíona
*Fíne*

*Wine* or *fair, beautiful*

Fíona could have been derived from two possible sources: the Latin *vinum* ('wine'), rendered *fíon* in modern Irish, or *fionn* ('fair', 'white', 'beautiful'). Fíona is often used as a shortened form of Lasairfhíona *(see page 40)*. Fíne was an abbess of Kildare, who died in 805.

## Fionnuala
*Fionnguala, Fionnghuala*  *Finola*

*Fair-shouldered*

In mythology, Fionnuala was the daughter of the sea god Lir. She and her brothers were turned into swans for 900 years by Aoife, their jealous stepmother. One Fionnghuala, with her husband, endowed the monastery of Donegal in 1474, in return for it being the burial place for them and their descendants. Fionnuala, mother of the sixteenth-century rebel chieftain Red Hugh O'Donnell, was considered the driving force behind his career. Nuala, the shortened form of Fionnuala, is very popular. Nola and Noleen are also abbreviated forms.

## Fionnúir
*Fionnabhair*  *Fennore*

*White sprite*

Notable women with this name were the daughter of the legendary queen of Connacht, Maeve, and the daughter of Conchobhar mac Nessa, the high king of Ulster. Its meaning is an obvious attraction.

## Gael

*Gaedheal*  *Gail, Gayle, Gaelle*

A name whose derivation and appeal are obvious, since the Gaels were the Celtic inhabitants of early Ireland and gave Ireland its language, Gaelic. They reached Ireland in about 700 BC, having spread eastwards from Central Europe, north of the Alps. *Gael* or *gaedheal* is sometimes used in Celtic communities as a name for a Gaelic speaker or a person from Ireland.

## Geraldine

*Gearóidín*

A popular name in Ireland, it originated with Lady Elizabeth FitzGerald from Kildare, a descendant of the Norman settlers, who was called 'the fair Geraldine' by a sixteenth-century courtier and poet, Surrey. The name has been popular ever since; in the nineteenth century it was widespread in all English-speaking countries. Ger is often used as a shortened form.

## Gormlaith

*Gormla*  *Illustrious princess*

This was a very popular name in early Ireland, particularly among royalty. Many famous women outlived their first husbands and remarried into other dynasties, including Gormlaith, daughter of the king of Leinster. She was first married to Olaf, the Viking leader of Dublin, and gave birth to a son, Sitric. She then married two high kings: Malachy and later Brian Boru.

# Grania
*Gráinne*

*She who inspires terror* or *corn goddess*

*Grace*

The best-known Gráinne was betrothed to the great warrior and founder of the Fianna, Fionn mac Cumhail, but eloped with one of his soldiers, Diarmaid. Fionn pursued them for 16 years, with Diarmaid leaving clues around the 'circuit of Ireland', in each place they spent the night, to suggest that he had not slept with her. Megalithic tombs thoughout the country are therefore known as 'Diarmaid and Gráinne's bed'. Gráinne was eventually reconciled with Fionn.

# Granuaile

Granuaile or Gráinne Ní Mháille (anglicised as Grace O'Malley) was a renowned sea captain who led 200 sea raiders from the Galway coast in the sixteenth century. She was twice widowed, twice imprisoned, fought Irish and English enemies, was condemned for piracy and finally pardoned by England's Queen Elizabeth I. She died in 1603. She was celebrated in verse and song, and in James Joyce's novel *Finnegan's Wake*. She is often seen as a poetic symbol for Ireland.

# Grian
*Greine*

*Sun, sun goddess*

Cnoc Greine, near Pallas Green (Pailis Greine), in Co. Limerick, is reputed to be the seat of Grian, the sun goddess. In legend, she is the daughter of Fionn; Loch Greine, in Co. Clare, is named after her.

# Hilde
*Battle*

*Hilda*

The name of a saintly Irish abbess (feast day: 18 November), and a name that was also made famous by St Hilda, the abbess of Whitby (614–680).

# Iseult

*Yseult, Isolt, Isolde*

In Arthurian legend, Iseult was the beautiful young Irish princess who was betrothed to the elderly king of Cornwall, Mark. Her mother prepared a love potion for her so she would be happy with the king, but Iseult shared it with his young nephew, Tristan, by mistake, and the two fell in love. Their story is the subject of one of Wagner's greatest operas, *Tristan and Isolde*.

# Isibéal

*Iseabeal, Sibéal*     *God is my oath*     *Isabel, Isabella, Sybil*

An Irish name based on Isabel, the Spanish form of Elizabeth, which was the name of John the Baptist's mother. All the European forms of the name come from the Hebrew name Elisheba, which means 'God is my oath'.

## Ita
*Íde, Íte*

*Thirst for goodness or knowledge*

*Ida*

St Ita was born in Co. Waterford about 480. She and St Brigid are the most influential female saints in early Irish Christianity. St Ita, whose name is said to refer to her hunger for God, was associated with education and founded an important convent in Kileedy, Co. Limerick. Kileedy means 'Ita's church'. One of her pupils was said to be St Brendan. She fasted excessively and is known as the 'foster mother of Irish saints'. She died at Kileedy in 570; her grave lies at the intersection of the nave and chancel of the church there. According to legend, she was Jesus's foster mother. Feast day: 15 January.

## Iuchra

In the Finn ballads, Iuchra is the daughter of Ábartach. He turns her rival, Aífe, into a heron.

## Joyce
*Seoighe*

*Lord*

*Joy*

This was an Anglo-Norman surname and the name of one of the Galway tribes. The original derivation was the Breton word for 'lord'. In the past, the name was used for boys; now it is an exclusively female name. It is also a surname, known the world over because of the Irish writer James Joyce.

# Kathleen

*Caitlín*

*(see Caitlín) Pure*

This is the Irish form of Catherine and has been used so often it has almost become a generic name for Irish girls abroad, for example in the song 'Take Me Home Again, Kathleen'. It came from France in the form Cateline, probably in relation to Catherine of Alexandria, and was introduced into Ireland by the Anglo-Normans. The Irish form is often shortened to Cáit.

# Keely

*Keeley, Keily, Kiely
(also Keela and Kyla)*

*Beautiful, graceful*

A contemporary name that may come from the girl's name Caoilfhionn (usual form Keelin) or may be a feminine form of the boy's name Kiely. In either case the derivation of the name is *cadhla* ('beautiful', 'graceful'), a word found mainly in poetry, so the name implies 'beauty that only poetry can capture'.

# Kelly

*Ceallach*

*Red-headed*

A name originally used for both girls and boys. Since the mid-twentieth century it has become a very popular girl's name in Britain, the United States, Canada and Australia, and for boys it is again growing in popularity. It was traditionally thought to mean 'church-goer', but more recent opinion holds that it was a much older name meaning 'red-headed'.

# Kerry

*Ciarrá*

*Land of the descendants of Ciar*

There was no letter 'k' in the Irish Gaelic alphabet. This is a modern Irish name, taken from Co. Kerry, one of Ireland's most beautiful west-coast counties, which means 'land of the descendants of Ciar'. Ciar was the son of the legendary queen Maeve of Connacht. Ciar means 'dark', so the name probably implied someone with dark hair and brown eyes. Kerry is increasing in popularity in Ireland and abroad.

# Kyna

A contemporary name with two possible sources: it may come from the Irish word *cion* ('love', 'affection', 'esteem') or from *ciona* ('best', 'champion', 'star').

## Laoise

*Laoiseach, Luighseach, Luigsech*    *Radiant girl*    *Lucy*

This name is probably derived from that of the god Lugh, and means 'radiant girl'. The feast day of St Luigsech, or Laoise, is celebrated on 22 May.

## Lára

*Loretta*    *Laurel*    *Laura*

The diminutive Loretta is sometimes used because it sounds like Loreto in Italy. Mary and Joseph's house in Nazareth, in which Jesus grew up, was said to have been miraculously transported to Loreto in the thirteenth century. It became the name of a nuns' teaching order: Mother Teresa of Calcutta was trained by the Irish sisters of Loreto.

## Lassarina

*Lasairfhíona, Lasairíona*    *Flame of the wine*

This is an ancient Irish name, very popular in Connacht in the late Middle Ages, and one regularly given to daughters of the O'Connor family. Fíona is a shortened form of Lasairfhíona. One famous woman with the name Lasairfhíona was the mother of Domnall Beg and 'head of the women of Leth-Cuinn'. She died in 1282.

## Líadan
*Líadain*
*Grey lady*

Líadan was a poet whose lover was the poet Cuirithir. On a whim, she rejected him and became a nun. Heartbroken, he became a monk. Both later bitterly regretted their actions. He was exiled and she died on the stone he knelt on to pray. One of her laments exists in a ninth-century manuscript. Another Líadan was the mother of St Ciarán of Seir. Legend has it that while asleep she turned her face to heaven and a star fell into her mouth. In this way she conceived Ciarán.

## Liban
*Lí Bhan, Lí Ban, Líobhan*
*Beauty of women*

In mythology, Lí Ban (also known as Muirgein), was a half-pagan, half-Christian woman, who lived in Lough Neagh for 300 years. She was eventually caught by a fisherman and became a Christian. In the Ulster tales, Lí Ban is Lúathlám's wife.

## Maeve
*Meadhbh, Maebh, Méabh*
*She who intoxicates*

The most famous woman with this name was Maeve, the warrior queen of Connacht. She left Conchobhar for her fourth husband, Ailill, and appears in Ireland's greatest epic, *Táin Bó Cuailgne* ('The Cattle Raid of Cooley'), in which she went to war with Ulster to gain Daire's great brown bull. The raid ended in the death of Cúchulainn, the Ulster warrior. The name was also that of the goddess of Tara, in Co. Meath, and wife of the legendary Art mac Cuinn. Maeve also appears as the fairy queen Mab in Shakespeare's *Romeo and Juliet*.

## Máire
*Máirín*
*Bitter*
*Mary*

Until the end of the fifteenth century, this name was not given to girls out of reverence for the Virgin Mary. Now it has become a very popular name for girls. The form Muire is used exclusively for the Virgin Mary. In 1532, Máire, the wife of O'Boyle, was thrown from her horse on her own doorstep and died. Máire ní Scolai (1909–85) was well known for collecting, interpreting and performing traditional Irish songs.

## Mairéad
*Máirghréad, Maighread, Maraid*
*Pearl*
*Margaret*

This name comes from the Greek *margaron* ('pearl') and has several forms. It was the name of many saints, including St Margaret of Antioch. It was brought to Europe by the Crusaders and introduced into Ireland by the Anglo-Normans, where it has remained very popular, with several forms. St Margaret was also the wife of Malcolm III of Scotland, who died in 1093. He was the son of Duncan; they were portrayed in Shakespeare's *Macbeth*. Mairéad is probably a diminutive of Máire (Mary).

# Majella

The Italian surname of St Gerard (1726–55), the patron saint of mothers and childbirth, who was canonised in 1904.

## Maolíosa
*Máelíosu*                          *Devotee of Christ*                          *Melissa*

A beautiful name most likely derived from *maol* ('devotee', 'follower') and *Íosa* ('Jesus'), which was initially used by clerics. From the tenth century on, however, its lay usage spread. The best-known bearer of the name was a religious lyric poet who died in 1086. A second possible source could be from the Gaelic word *mil* ('honey'). There are many Irish legends about saints who were beekeepers, so it might have started as a nickname. Originally, it was a boy's name but is now used for girls.

## Meara
*Sea*

A pretty name that probably comes from the Gaelic word *mara* ('sea').

## Molly
*Mallaidh*

A pet name for Mary, which has appeared in Irish songs and stories for over 300 years (e.g. Molly Malone). An Irish form was found for it because it had become so widespread.

## Mona

*Muadhnait, Muadnat*

*Noble, good*

This attractive name is popular in Ireland and probably used there more often than anywhere else in the world. Several possible derivations have been mooted. It may come from the Gaelic *muadhnait* ('noble'); from the French name Monique ('giver of advice'), introduced by the Normans; or from a shortened form of Madonna ('lady'), as in the Mona Lisa. St Muadhnait of Drumcliffe, Co. Sligo, was sister to St Molaise, who founded a monastery at Devenish. Her feast day: 6 January.

## Mór

*Móire*

*Great one*

An ancient Irish name that was the most popular female name in medieval Ireland. The name of a goddess whose descendants became the kings and queens of Munster, it was also a reverential substitute for the name of the Virgin Mary. Mór Mumhan, considered a paragon among Irish women of her time, was the wife of Finghin, king of Munster. She died in 631. Mór, the daughter of Mac Cába, was described as 'the nurse of the learned and destitute of Ireland'. She died in 1527.

## Mughain

*Young maiden*

The name of a goddess and two saints, which comes from the south of Ireland.

### Muireann
*Mairenn*
*Sea-white, sea-fair*

This is an ancient Irish name. In mythology, Muireann was Oisín's wife. It was also the name of Cael's nurse; he was a Fianna warrior. Muireann composed a poem that won him Credhe, the daughter of the king of Kerry. Another Muireann was the wife of a king of Connacht, Raghallach mac Fuatach, who killed his nephew and was told that he himself would be killed by his own children. Their daughter was brought up by a pious woman and became the fairest woman in Ireland. The king, who did not know she was his daughter, fell in love with her and was beaten to death as a result. Muireann later married the high king, Diarmaid.

### Muírgheal
*Muirgel*
*Bright as the sea*
*Meryl, Muriel, Merrill*

A name that was popular in all Celtic regions in the Middle Ages and then fell from favour. It is now becoming popular again. It was the name of a ninth-century wife of the king of Leinster, and of the daughter of the high king Máel Sechnaill I. The latter lived to be very old and died in 926 at Clonmacnoise.

### Muirne
*Murine*
*High-spirited*
*Myrna, Morna*

In Irish mythology, Muirne was the mother of the great warrior, Fionn mac Cumhail. She gave birth to him after her husband died, and left him in the care of a female druid and a female warrior.

## Nábla

*Nápla, Náible*

*Lovable*

*Annabel*

A name with a Latin origin that was brought into Ireland by the Normans, probably in the forms Amabel, Anable and Anaple, all related to the French *aimable* ('lovable', 'beloved'); the initial vowel was lost in the Irish forms.

## Naomh

*A saint*

This is one of several Irish words that have recently been converted into first names. The ancient lists of saints, the martyrologies, were often accused of 'inventing saints out of place names', so there seems to be a precedent for doing so.

## Neala

*Neila, Neilla, Nelda*

*Female champion*

A modern feminine form of the boy's name Niall, it means 'female champion'. It is seen most often in the USA, especially among people whose ancestors came from Northern Ireland, where the allied surnames Neal, Neill, McNeill and O'Neill are commonplace.

## Néamhain

*Nemon*

*Battle fury*

This was the name of an Irish war goddess in ancient times.

# Nessa
*Nease, Neas, Ness*
*Not gentle*

Nessa was Conchobhar's mother. She persuaded her second husband, Fergus, to make Conchobhar king of Ulster for a year, which also increased her own power. Conchobhar ruled so wisely that the people would not allow him to return the kingdom to Fergus. A sister of St Ita also had the name.

# Niamh
*Niam*
*Radiance, brightness*

The Celtic goddess Niamh Chinn Óir ('Niamh of the Golden Hair') was one of the daughters of the sea god Lir. She seduced Oisín, the warrior Fionn's son, and carried him off on her horse to the Land of Promise. Oisín pined for Ireland, and returned on a magic horse Niamh had provided. She warned him not to dismount, and when he fell off the horse by accident he found that 300 years had passed and he had turned into a blind old man.

# Noelle
*Nodhlaig, Nollaig*
*Christmas*

The feminine form of Noel, given to a child born at Christmas. The name has only been used in Ireland since the early twentieth century.

# Nonín
*Daisy*

The Irish word for 'daisy', which has only been used as a first name in fairly recent times. Its pretty form and meaning look likely to make it a favourite.

# Nora

*Nóra*     *Honour*     *Norah*

This popular name is the shortened form of Onóra, the Irish form of the Latin Honora, which was introduced into Ireland by the Anglo-Normans. It was quite popular in medieval Ireland, particularly among the O'Briens: three O'Brien daughters had the name between 1579 and 1600. Noreen is a popular diminutive; its Irish form is Nóirín.

# Órla

*Órlaith, Orfhlaith, Orlagh*     *Golden princess*

One of a series of princesses' names, this was the fourth most popular name in twelfth-century Ireland, when it was the name of a sister and a niece of Brian Boru, the high king. Tiarnán O'Ruairc, king of Breifne, who lost his wife Dervorguilla to Diarmaid mac Murrough, had a daughter called Órlaith. The name fell out of favour in the Middle Ages, but is now very popular again.

# Orna

*Odharnait, Órnait*     *Dark-haired*

This unusual name is the female form of the boy's name Oran and comes from the word *odhra* ('dark-haired'). It is the name of several saints: one may have established a Christian settlement on Iona before St Columba.

# Patricia

*Pádraigín, Paidrigín*
*Noble*

The female equivalent of Patrick (Pádraig), Ireland's patron saint, whose name was derived from the Latin Patricius. There are records of a St Patricia of Naples, who lived in the seventh century. The name began to be used in Ireland in the early twentieth century, possibly because it was the name of one of the granddaughters of Britain's Queen Victoria, Princess Patricia of Connacht.

# Philomena
*Powerful friend, loved one*

A name with Greek origins, its popularity in Ireland relates to the cult of St Philomena, whose relics were thought to have been found in Rome in 1802. Their authenticity was subsequently challenged; the Vatican suppressed her cult in 1960.

# Proinnséas

*Próinséas, Proinnsias,*
*Pronsaisín*
*Frances*

A popular name in Ireland today, adopted in honour of St Francis of Assisi (1181–1226), the patron saint of birds and animals. The boy's name Proinsias, an Irish form of Francis (*see page 102*), was taken from the Latin Franciscus ('Frenchman'), and this female form has the same root. It was said that St Francis was given the name because he learned French so readily. The female form of the name belonged to a saintly Roman widow: her feast day is 9 March. The earliest examples of the name in England date from the fifteenth century. It probably passed from England to Ireland at a later period. The form with '-*ín*' is sometimes anglicised as Frankie.

# Radha
*Vision* or *red*

The name has become popular in Ireland because of its link with *radharc* ('vision'). It may also be connected with *ruadh* ('red'), so it would be a perfect name for a red-haired girl.

# Ranait
*Rathnait, Rathnat*       *Grace, prosperity*

St Rathnait is the patron saint of Kilraghts, Co. Antrim (feast day: 5 August).

# Realtán
*Reailtín*       *Star*       *Stella*

The Irish form of Stella, taken from the Latin word for 'star'. Its lovely meaning must recommend it as a girl's name.

# Regan
*Ríoghán, Rígán*       *The king's child*

A name that can be used for a girl or boy, it comes from the diminutive of *rí* ('king', 'sovereign'). It may also be related to the Irish surname O'Regan, which means 'descendant of a king'.

# Ríbh
*Stripe*

In contemporary rural mythology, Ríbh is associated with a striped cat (the modern Irish word for 'stripe' is *riabh*). If Ríbh lets you stroke the cat, it is said that you'll have good luck.

## Ríoghnach
*Ríghnach, Ríonach, Ríona*    *Queenly*                    *Regina*

Ríoghnach was the wife of Niall of the Nine Hostages, and mother of
Laeghaire, Énna, Maine, Eoghan, two Conalls and Cairbre. She and her
husband founded a dynasty: it was predicted that 'thine and thy
children's for ever the kingdom and supreme power shall be'. They are
the ancestors of the O'Neills, MacLoughlins, O'Donnells, O'Gallaghers,
O'Gormleys and other northern Irish families. Two of their children, a
Conall and Eoghan, have left their influence in the names of Irish
counties. Ríoghnach is also an Irish saint, the sister of St Finnian of
Clonard (her feast day: 18 December). Another saint with the same name
has her feast day on 9 February.

## Ríomthach
*Ríofach, Ríomhthach*

Ríomthach was the name of one of five sisters who founded a church at
Killiney, Co. Dublin, called Cill Inghean Léinín ('the church of the
daughters of Léníne') in the sixth century. Their brother was St Colman
of Cloyne, Co. Cork.

## Ríona
*Rionach*    *Like a queen*

A lovely name that comes from *ríon* ('queen'). Mary, the mother of Christ,
is Ríona's special patron, so she has several feast days, including
25 March, 15 August and 8 September.

# Róisín
*Horse* or *little rose*

Rose

Thought to be derived from the Old German *hros* ('horse'), it has also been connected with the Latin *rosa* ('rose') from earliest times. The name was introduced into Ireland by the Anglo-Normans. Róisín Dubh has been used as a poetic name for Ireland for five centuries. The poet James Clarence Mangan (1803–49) translated a sixteenth-century poem of the same name as 'Dark Rosaleen'. St Rose of Lima was so-called because of the rose-like appearance of her face as a child. Róisín is a diminutive of Róis, which was a popular name for a woman in Ireland long before St Rose was born.

# Ruarí
*Red-headed ruler*

Rori

From *rua* and *rí* ('red-headed ruler'), this is now used as the feminine form of the boy's name Rory.

# Ryanne

Derived from *rí* and the diminutive *-in*, meaning 'little king', this name is appearing in the USA as a female form of Ryan.

# Saoirse
*Freedom, liberty*

This is a contemporary example of the adoption of an Irish word as a personal name: it has an obvious appeal. It began to be used in the 1920s (the Irish Free State in the south came into being in 1922) and gained impetus when that became the Republic of Ireland in 1949. It can be used for both boys and girls, but is usually a female name.

# Sceanbh
*Spike*

This unusual name seems to be derived from the Gaelic word *sceanbh* ('spike') and belonged to the wife of a harpist, Craiftine. His harp could either inspire warriors to brave feats or send them to sleep. While her husband was playing, Sceanbh fell in love with Cormac, son of the king of Ulster, Conchobhar.

# Seosaimhín
*God shall add*　　　　*Josephine*

The Irish version of Josephine, this name has French origins. It became popular in France because it was the name of the Emperor Napoleon's wife. It is the feminine form of the Hebrew name Joseph, which means 'God shall add', a name that has been revered in Celtic communities since Christianity was introduced.

# Shannon

*Shannyn, Channon, Shanyn*

The River Shannon is Ireland's longest river, and is probably named after an early Celtic god or goddess. The root of the name is *sen* or *sean* ('old'), so it means 'old one'. It was not often used as a first name in Ireland, but became popular among Irish immigrants to the United States, Canada and Australia in the 1930s. It is still very popular there, and particularly so in Britain.

# Shauna

*God is gracious*

A very popular contemporary name in Ireland at present, it is the feminine form of Sean (the Irish form of John), which means 'God is gracious'.

# Sheenagh

*God is gracious*      *Sheena*

An Irish form of Jane, which itself is a feminine form of John, hence its meaning. It has also been suggested that it could be a form of Sinéad.

# Sibéal

*Wise woman*      *Sybil*

One of the many non-Irish names for which Irish versions were found at the time of the Gaelic revival at the beginning of the twentieth century. It is the Irish equivalent of Isabel, which itself was the Spanish form of Elizabeth.

# Síle
*Pure and musical*    Sheila, Sheela, Sheelagh

A name that comes from the Roman family name Cecilia and was brought to Ireland by the Anglo-Normans. St Cecilia is the patron saint of music. The name may also have been influenced by the Hebrew name Shelah ('longed for'). Síle, the wife of Niall, son of Art O'Neill, was in Omagh Castle in 1471 when it was besieged and captured by Henry O'Neill.

# Sinead
*Sinéad, Seonaid*        *Jane*

This name was introduced into Ireland by the Anglo-Normans as Jehanne, a female form of John. One of the most famous people with this name was Sinéad Flanagan, born in Balbriggan, Co. Dublin, in 1878. A teacher, she taught Irish for the Gaelic League, where one of her pupils was Éamon de Valera, a mathematics teacher and the future president of Ireland. They were married in 1910. She also wrote plays, poems and fairy stories for children.

# Siobhan
*Siobhán, Sibán*        *Lily*        *Joan*

Introduced by the Anglo-Normans and very popular ever since, this was probably a form of the French Jehanne, a feminine form of John. One of Ireland's most famous actresses was Siobhán McKenna (1923–86). She was born in Belfast and moved to Galway with her family when she was five. She acted in the Taibhdhearc, Galway's Irish language theatre, and joined the Abbey Theatre, Dublin, in 1944. She was declared 'Actress of the Year' in 1958. Another notable namesake was Sibán, daughter of the third Earl of Desmond and wife of Tadg mac Carthaig, said to be 'the most celebrated wine-bibber of his age'.

## Sive
*Sadb, Sadhbh, Saidhbhe*          *Sally*
*Sweetness, goodness*

An ancient Irish name and that of Oisín's mother. She spent part of her life as a fawn because of a spell that had been cast by the Dark Druid, a long-time enemy of the Fianna, the band of warriors. Sadb Sulbair ('of the pleasant speech') was the daughter of Ailill and Maeve, the goddess-queen of Connacht. Other famous women with this name include the wife of the legendary Munster king, Ailill Ólom; Brian Boru's daughter, who died in 1048; and the king of Thomond's wife.

## Sorcha
*Brightness, light*          *Sarah, Sally*

An old Irish name that was popular in the Middle Ages and remained so until the nineteenth century, when its use declined. It is now becoming popular again in Britain and Ireland.

## Súsanna
*Lily*

This name is the Irish form of the old Hebrew name Susannah. There are also two pet forms: Sósaidh (Susie) and Siú (Sue).

# Taillte

*Tailltiu*

Taillte was the daughter of mac ú Moir in Irish legend and gave her name to Mag Taillten (now Teltown), Co. Meath, where Aonach Taillteann, an ancient assembly, was held at the beginning of August, presided over by the king of Tara. It is a prehistoric cemetery, where games to honour the dead were held. The last assembly was held in 1168, presided over by Ruaidhrí O'Connor. In this way he asserted his claim to the high kingship. The 'Teltown Marriages', thought to be a relic of the old assembly, survived till the eighteenth or nineteenth century. Couples were married in a ring-fort there. If the marriage ran into trouble, they could dissolve it by returning to the fort, standing back to back in the middle, with one then walking south and the other north.

# Tallula

*Tuilelaith, Tailefhlaith*
*Abundance of sovereignty,*
*lady of abundance*

There were two saints of this name in the eighth and ninth centuries, both abbesses: one of Clonguffin, Co. Meath (died 782); the other of Kildare (died 885; feast day: 6 January). Twilleliah was the anglicised form favoured in the seventeenth century. Tallulah Bankhead, the famous early-twentieth-century American film star, had another form of the name, though in her case it may have come from the Tallulah Falls in Georgia.

## Tara
*Teamhair, Temair*          *Eminence, elevated place*

In legend, Teamhair is the wife of an early Irish chieftain, but the name
also comes from the royal prehistoric site in Teamhair (Tara), Co. Meath.
By 500 BC the site had become the central focus of royal and religious
power in Ireland, and was the place where the high kings of Ireland
were anointed. Temair was the name of the wife of the high king
Diarmaid Rúanaid, who died in 665. Through Margaret Mitchell's novel
*Gone with the Wind*, and the subsequent film, the name has become
internationally popular.

## Teagan
*Tegan*          *Beautiful*

This unusual name is the Irish form of the Welsh name Tegwen (or
Tegwyn), which means 'beautiful', so it needs no further
recommendation as a name for a baby girl.

## Teffia
*Teaffa*

An example of a place name, Teffia, in Co. Longford, being used as a first
name. It was the name of a woman associated with the site.

## Treasa
*Treise*          *Strength*          *Theresa, Teresa*

An old Irish name, this is the Irish form of Theresa or Teresa. It is a very
popular name in Ireland because of two inspirational saints: the
Carmelite nun St Theresa of Avila (1515–82) and St Theresa of Lisieux
(1873–97). There is also a link with the Irish word *treise* ('strength'),
which is another reason for the name's popularity.

# Tuathla
*Princess of the people*

A feminine form of the male name Tuathal, its meaning makes it a popular name. Tuathla was a queen of Leinster in the eighth century.

# Uaine
*Green, verdant*

In the Finn legends, Uaine Buide is an enchanting musician, who is accompanied by all the birds in the Land of Promise.

# Uallach
*Proud*

This was the name of the chief poetess of Ireland. She was the daughter of Muimnechán, and died in 934.

## Ultana
### *An Ulsterwoman*

A name used mainly in Northern Ireland as a female form of Ultán ('an Ulsterman'). The name was popular in the early period, with 18 saints of the name, including the most famous, St Ultán, the seventh-century abbot, bishop and scholar of Ardbraccan, Co. Meath. He was known for his care of the poor, orphans and the sick and is the patron saint of Ireland's children. A hospital in Dublin is named after him. Another name for the Ardbraccan monastery was Ultán's Well. It was said that St Ultán 'fed with his own hands every child in Erin who had no support', particularly children of women who died of plague. His scholarly works included a poem and a life of St Brigid. His feast day: 4 September.

## Una
*Úna*  *Oonagh, Oona*

In legend, Úna was the mother of Conn of the Hundred Battles. It was a popular name in medieval Ireland. Úna MacDermott is the subject of the seventeenth-century song, 'Úna Bhán' ('Fair Úna'). A poet, Tomás Láidir Costello, fell in love with her. She was much richer than he was and her parents disapproved. Úna started to waste away, but when Tomás visited her she began to recover. He made a promise to wait no longer than half an hour before crossing a stream on the way home, and had just crossed it when he was called back. Because of his vow, he did not return and Úna died. She was buried on an island in Lough Key and he swam out to the island on three successive nights, mourning her in the words of the tragic song.

# Boys' names Λ το Z

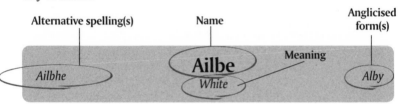

Alternative spelling(s)          Name          Anglicised form(s)

*Ailbhe*          **Ailbe**          Meaning          *Alby*

*White*

This name is found in both pagan and Christian contexts. St Ailbe of Emly, Co. Tipperary, a bishop of Rome, who died in 527 (feast day: 12 September), helped to bring Christianity to southern Ireland. He was a near contemporary of St Patrick, so was known as 'that other Patrick of the island of Ireland'. Ailbe can also be used as a female name.

Description

## Áengus

*Óengus, Aonghus,*
*Aongus*

*One choice, sole strength*

*Angus*

This ancient name was once very common. Five saints are among those with the name, including Óengus Céile Dé (feast day: 11 March), as well as kings, warriors and poets, including Óengus mac Óengusa, the 'chief poet of Ireland', who died in 932. In Celtic mythology, Áengus was the god of youth and love, and the son of Dagda and Boann, after whom the River Boyne was named. He helped lovers, including Diarmaid and Gráinne.

## Aidan

*Aodhán, Áedán*

*Little flame*

This is a diminutive of Aodh. Several saints had this name, the most famous being Aidan of Lindisfarne, who was sent to convert the Anglo-Saxons in Northumbria, after serving as a monk on Iona. He established a monastery on the island of Lindisfarne, which became the centre for spreading Christianity throughout the north of England.

## Ailbe

*Ailbhe*

*White*

*Alby*

This name is found in both pagan and Christian contexts. St Ailbe of Emly, Co. Tipperary, a bishop of Rome, who died in 527 (feast day: 12 September), helped to bring Christianity to southern Ireland. He was a near contemporary of St Patrick, so was known as 'that other Patrick of the island of Ireland'. Ailbe can also be used as a female name.

# Ailill
*Beauty* or *rocky place*

A name with two possible sources: it may be derived from the Irish word *áilleacht* ('beauty') or from *aileach* ('rocky place'). Ailill was the young husband of Queen Maeve. She chose him, she said, because he was 'a man without meanness, fear or jealousy, a match for my own greatness'. His argument with her over who had the greater herd of cattle led to the Cattle Raid of Cooley, one of the greatest epic tales in Irish mythology. Maeve needed the Brown Bull of Cooley to win the argument, so she went to war to get it.

# Aindrias
*Andriú*                    *Brave, manly, virile*                    *Andrew*

The Irish form of the name of the Christian apostle Andrew, the first apostle called by Jesus. The name comes from the Greek Andreas, and has been popular in Celtic communities since the introduction of Christianity.

# Alastar
*Alusdar, Alusdrann*                    *Defender of man*                    *Alastair, Alaisdair*

The Irish form of the Greek name Alexander, the name was introduced into Scotland by Queen Margaret in the twelfth century. Contact between Ireland and Scotland brought it into Northern Ireland, where it became very popular with Irish people of Scots descent.

# Alroy
*Red*

This name would be appropriate for a red-headed boy since it is taken from the Irish word *rua*, which means 'red'.

## Aodh

*Áed, Aodha, Aoidh*

*Fire*

*Hugh*

An ancient and very common Irish name, this was a favourite among the O'Connors of Connacht and the O'Neills and O'Donnells of Ulster. Hugh O'Neill, the Earl of Tyrone, and Red Hugh O'Donnell, the Earl of Tyrconnell, led a rebellion and defeated the forces of Elizabeth I of England, before being defeated at the Battle of Kinsale in 1601. It is also the name of high kings and many saints, including Áed mac Bricc of Rahugh, Co. Westmeath. His oratory on Slieve League, Co. Donegal, is still a place of pilgrimage on 10 November each year. The abbot of Terryglass, Co. Tipperary, Áed Cruamthainn, compiled *The Book of Leinster* between 1151 and 1224, which is said to 'sum up all the learning of the monastic period of Irish writing'.

## Árdal

*Ardghal, Ardal*

*Great valour, notable warrior*

*Arnold*

A favourite name in Ulster, most commonly among the MacKenna, MacArdle and MacMahon families, who anglicised it as Arnold. It probably comes from a combination of the words *árd* and *geal* ('high courage').

## Ardan

*High aspiration*

A name taken from the Irish word *ardanach*, which means 'high aspiration'. Ardan was one of the three sons of Usna, an Ulster chieftain. Deirdre had fallen in love with one of his brothers, Naoise, and Ardan helped them escape to Scotland so she would not be forced to marry the king of Ulster, Conchobhar mac Nessa, to whom she was betrothed. They were tricked into returning to Ireland and all three brothers were treacherously murdered.

## Art
### Bear

An ancient Irish personal name that comes from the old Irish word for 'bear', an animal sacred to the Celts. It is used here in the sense of 'outstanding warrior' or 'champion'. One of the earliest people to bear the name was Art Óenfer (Art the Lonely), a pagan high king, a semi-mythical figure, and father of Cormac mac Airt (Conn of the Hundred Battles). His father's mistress was a demoted goddess called Becuma. She was jealous of Art and sent him on a quest to find a beautiful young woman called Delbchaem. Art rescued her after overcoming many dangers and banished Becuma. Art ruled so honestly that two angels hovered over him in battle.

## Barra
*Bairrfhionn, Barrfind, Bairrionn*    **Fair-haired, fair-headed**    *Barry*

The name of eight saints, including the patron saint of Cork and Barrfhionn of Kilbarron, Co. Donegal. The latter's voyage to the Land of Promise encouraged St Brendan the Navigator to undertake his great journey. The name was a shortened form of Bartholomew, from the time when biblical names were common. It is a name in its own right, but is often used as a pet form of Finnbarr and Barrfinn.

# Bearach

*Berach*

*Spear, javelin* hence *pointed, sharp*

*Barry*

This was a fairly common name in early Ireland and that of several saints, including St Berach, the abbot of Bangor (feast day: 21 April). Another St Berach, who lived in the sixth century, is the patron saint of Kilbarry, Co. Roscommon. He was one of the royal line of Connacht and is the patron saint of the O'Hanlys, who used his name as a family name until the nineteenth century, when they anglicised it as Barry.

# Bradan

*Salmon*

*Braden*

The Irish word *bradan* means 'salmon'. The Salmon of Knowledge, the Bradan Feasa, appears in Irish legend, and is central to the story of Fionn mac Cumhail, the great warrior of the Fianna, and one of the most important people in Irish mythology. The Fianna was a band of chieftains, warriors, musicians, poets, priests and physicians.

# Bran

*A raven*

This was one of the most popular names in early Ireland and used by the O'Byrnes until after the Middle Ages. In the Finn tales, two warriors in the Fianna have the name. St Bran is the patron saint of Clane, Co. Kildare (feast day: 18 May). Bran Finn, who died in 671, was a famous king and poet, and Bran was also the name of Fionn mac Cumhaill's wolfhound.

# Brendan

*Breandán, Brénainn,*
*Bréanainn*

*Prince*

A very popular name, originally said to have come from Wales. It is the
name of many Irish saints, including St Breandán of Birr, but the most
celebrated is Brendan the Navigator (died 577), who undertook a seven-
year journey of discovery. He was said to have been the first European
to reach America. His voyage is the subject of a classic medieval tale,
*The Voyage of St Brendan*, translated into almost every European
language. Thought to have been born near Tralee, Co. Kerry, he founded
monasteries at Ardfert, Co. Kerry, and Clonfert, Co. Galway.
His feast day: 16 May.

# Brennan

*Braonán, Braon, Bren*

*Drop of water* or *tear*

Derived from *braon* ('drop of water', hence 'tear'), this name is mostly
used as a surname in Ireland, but is now appearing as a first name in the
United States.

# Brian

*High, noble*

A name thought to be Celtic in origin, and made famous by Ireland's
most celebrated king, Brian Boru. He was acknowledged as Ireland's
high king in 1002 and defeated the Norseman at the Battle of Clontarf in
1014. He united warring dynasties and broke the Viking hold on Ireland,
but died in the battle. In mythology, Brian was the eldest of Tureann's
three sons, the Celtic equivalents of the Greek Argonauts.

# Cabhán
*Cavan, Kevan, Keevan*

This Gaelic name comes from the Irish word *cabhán*, which means 'grassy hill' or 'hollow', but it is usually associated with the name of the Ulster county, Co. Cavan.

# Cahal
*Cathal*
*Strong in battle*

A popular name in the Middle Ages, borne by kings of Munster and Connacht. In modern times it was popularised by Cathal Brughal (1874–1922), an Irish Republican and politician. Born in Dublin, he joined the Gaelic League and in 1913 became a lieutenant in the Irish Volunteers. He was second in command during the 1916 Easter Rising, and was severely wounded. He served as Minister of Defence between 1919 and 1922, and died of wounds sustained fighting in the civil war.

# Canice
*Coinneach*
*Attractive or pleasant person*
*Kenneth, Kenny*

The Irish word *coinneach* means 'attractive or pleasant person'. St Coinneach was a sixth-century Irish missionary who founded churches in Ireland, Scotland and Wales. The church he established in Kilkenny, Cill Coinneach ('Coinneach's church'), gave the town its name. It is now renowned as a centre for Irish art and craft.

# Carney
*Cearnaigh, Cearney, Kearney*
*Victorious champion*

This name is derived from the Gaelic word *cearnach* ('victorious'), which implies 'victorious champion'.

# Carrick
### A rock

*Carrig*  *Craig*

A name with a straightforward derivation: it is taken from the Irish word *carraig*, which means 'a rock'. It would be a fine name for a boy with a strong, steady character.

# Casey
### Vigilant in war

Derived from an early Irish name, Cathasach ('vigilant in war'), this name has been used in recent times as a first name in Ireland and the United States. It is used for both boys and girls. It became famous in the twentieth century because of Jonathan Luther 'Casey' Jones (1863–1900), the engine driver on the Cannonball Express in America, who saved his passengers by sacrificing his own life.

# Cearbhall
### Fierce warrior

*Cearúl, Cearúil*  *Carroll, Carl, Karl*

An ancient name taken directly from the Gaelic word *cearbhall*, which means 'brave in fighting' or 'valorous in battle', hence 'fierce warrior'.

# Cian
### Ancient, enduring

 *Kean*

This was the name of several legendary figures, including Cian, son of the god of medicine. He seduced Ethlínn, the daughter of Balor, who was imprisoned in a tower. Their son was Lugh, the sun god, the father of the Ulster warrior Cúchulainn. It was also the name of the son-in-law of the high king Brian Boru; both were killed at the Battle of Clontarf in 1014.

## Ciarán
*Black*

*Kieran, Kieron*

A very popular name and that of many saints, including Ciarán the Elder, patron saint of Ossory, Co. Offaly. He founded a monastery there, which became the burial place of the kings of Ossory. It is said that a wild boar helped him build his cell by cutting branches with its tusks. (His feast day: 5 March.) The most famous bearer of the name was the abbot of the great monastery of Clonmacnoise, Co. Offaly, which he founded in 547. It became an unrivalled centre of Irish art and literature, retaining its power and influence until the 1550s. (His feast day: 9 September.)

## Cillian
*Cillín, Cilléne, Killian*
*Associated with the church*
or *good sense*

The name of a famous Irish saint, who was born in Cavan and martyred, with other Irish missionaries, at Wurtzburg in Germany in about 689, by Geilana, the wife of Duke Gozbert. It may come from the word *cill* ('church') and mean 'associated with the church', or from *ciall* ('good sense').

## Clancy
*Red-headed warrior*

An example of a contemporary Irish surname now used as a first name, particularly in the United States. It comes from the Irish words *flann* and *cath*, which mean 'red (-headed) warrior'. The surname came from *mac Fhlannchaidh* ('son of the red warrior').

## Cleary
*Clearie*
*Minstrel, scholar*

Another example of an Irish surname now being used as a first name, it is derived from the word *cliareach* ('minstrel', 'scholar').

*Cluny*

# Clooney
*Grassy meadow*

*Keeper*

A Gaelic name that has two possible sources: it may be derived from the Irish word *cluain* ('grassy meadow'), or could be connected with an Irish word that sounds similar and means 'flattery'. It is usually a surname, but is now also being used as a first name for boys and girls, a common practice in Ireland.

# Cody
*Prosperous*

A name derived from the surname *mac Óda* ('son of Otto'). Otto was an old German name signifying prosperity. Cody is popular in the United States as a boy's name, but is increasingly also used there as a girl's name.

# Coilin
*Little chieftain*

*Colin*

A name derived from the Irish word *coll* ('chieftain'), it is used here with the diminutive *-in*, and so means 'little chieftain'. Its meaning is an obvious attraction.

71

# Colman
*Little dove*

A name with the same root as Colm (*see below*), it means 'little dove' and has developed into a name in its own right. One of hundreds of saints with this name was St Colman of Kilmacduagh, who lived as a recluse until he met the king of Connacht. As the king sat down to dinner on Easter Sunday, the feast was spirited away. The king followed it and found a weakened St Colman devouring it after his Lenten fast.

# Colum
*Colm, Columb*      *Dove*      *Columba*

The most famous saint bearing this name is Columcille ('dove of the church'). His guardian angel allowed him to choose his virtues: he chose virginity and wisdom. Because he had chosen the right ones, he was also given the gift of prophecy. He founded several monasteries in Ireland, including, in 546, Doire Cholm Cille, which became modern Londonderry. He then founded the monastery on Iona, in Scotland, where he died in 597. His biography was written by the abbot who succeeded him. His feast day: 9 June.

# Conall
*Connall*      *Strong as a wolf or hound*      *Connell*

A name given to early kings and warriors. In legend, Conall Cearnach (Conall the Victorious) was a great warrior who avenged the death of his foster brother Cúchulainn. He was also said to have been Ireland's representative at Christ's crucifixion and one of the people who closed his tomb with a rock and rolled it back on the first Easter Day.

## Conn
*Wisdom, reason*

In mythology, Conn was one of the children of Lir, who were turned into swans by Aoife, their stepmother. The legendary ancestor of the kings of Ireland and many noble Irish families was Conn of the Hundred Battles. He reigned from 177 to 212 and gave his name to the province of Connacht.

## Conor
*Conchúr, Conchobhar, Conchobar*     *Wolf lover, lover of hounds*     Connor

A name that has been popular in Ireland for centuries. It is taken from the old name Conchobhar and has been shortened and altered with usage. Conchobhar mac Nessa was a legendary king of Ulster. Fergus mac Róich, an exiled hero, said of him: 'This is how Conchobhar spends his time of sovereignty: one third of the day watching the youth, another third playing chess, another third drinking ale till he falls asleep from it. Though we have been exiled by him, I still maintain there is not in Ireland a warrior more wonderful.'

## Corey
*Corie, Cory, Corry*

A name thought to have been derived in Ireland through a variety of surnames that included the root *corra* ('spear'). It may also have been used in Ireland because of its similarity to the Gaelic *cuairteoir* ('visitor'). Ireland has a tradition of hospitality to visitors, known or unknown. It has been popular in the United States as a first name since the 1960s.

# Cormac
### *Charioteer* or *son of Corb*

An ancient Irish name borne by kings, saints and warriors, including Cormac mac Airt, one of the legendary high kings of Ireland. The king of Munster, Cormac mac Carthaig, built Cormac's Chapel in Cashel, Co. Tipperary, and was killed in 1138. Cormac mac Cuilennáin was a king, bishop and scholar. He was killed on the battlefield in 908, defeated by the forces of Leinster. His book, *Cormac's Glossary*, is an important work on Irish language, and also contains articles on antiquities, history and mythology. In the seventeenth century, many Irish families changed the name to Charles, after Charles I of England.

# Crónán
*Cronin, Croney*
### *Dark-skinned, sallow*

A name that is probably derived from *crón* ('dark-skinned', 'sallow'). Several saints have this name, but the best-known is St Crónán, who lived in the seventh century and worked with the poor, the homeless and with travellers. He founded a monastery in a remote area of Tipperary, where he was born, but travellers found it hard to find, so he built a new one closer to the roadside. It became the modern town of Roscrea. In north Tipperary, the form Croney is still a traditional name among the O Hogans.

# Dáibhí

*Dáithí, Daibhead, Dahey*  
*Swiftness, nimbleness*  
*David, Davey*

The Irish form of the biblical name David, the king of the Israelites. Dáithí was the name of the last pagan king of Ireland, who ruled from 405 to 426, and was said to have had 24 sons. With Crimhthan the Great and Niall of the Nine Hostages, he led Irish fleets to raid the Roman Empire. He was killed by lightning in the Alps and is buried under a standing stone called King Dáithí's Stone. There is debate over its location: it is said to be in Co. Roscommon or on the Aran Islands, off the coast of Co. Galway. Another bearer of the name, the bishop of Armagh and papal legate of Ireland, who died in 550, has his name recorded in Latin, as Davidus. The name is also used as a surname.

# Dáire
*Fruitful, fertile*

Dáire is one of the commonest names in Irish legend and mythology, and may have been the name of a god of fertility or a bull god. Donn Cuailgne, the Brown Bull of Cooley, belonged to Dáire mac Fiachna. Dáire's refusal to hand the bull over on a year's loan of 50 heifers to Maeve, the warrior queen of Connacht, was one of the causes of the great battle of Táin Bó Cuailgne between the Ulstermen and the men of Ireland. One saint with the name was a woman (feast day: 8 August), so like many early Irish names, it may have been used by both men and women.

# Dálaigh

*Dálach*  
*Counsellor*  
*Daley, Daly*

A name that comes from the Irish word *dalach*, which means 'frequenter of gatherings', hence a counsellor or someone who attends meetings. The name also has connections with the word *dáil* ('meeting', 'gathering'). The Irish parliament is called the Dáil. Daley Thompson, the late-twentieth-century Olympic decathlete, helped make the name popular. It is also very common as a surname.

## Declan

*Deaglán, Declán*

*Light, gleam*

St Declan is the patron saint of Ardmore, Co. Waterford, where he founded a monastery. He is thought to have been one of the earliest Christian missionaries in Ireland, possibly preaching there before St Patrick. He was consecrated by the Pope in Rome, and is said to have met St Patrick on his way back to Ireland. He is reputed to have received a small bell from heaven, which found him a ship and accompanied him on his journey home. It pointed out where he was to build his monastery. An annual pilgrimage is held on his feast day: 24 July.

## Dermot

*Diarmaid, Diarmait, Diarmuid*

*Freeman*

An ancient name and that of several saints. In Celtic mythology, Diarmaid was the greatest lover in Irish literature. He and Gráinne fled from her husband, Fionn mac Cumhail, who pursued them for 16 years. Historically, it was the name of famous kings: Diarmait mac Cerbaill, the last great pagan king in Ireland, and the high king Diarmait Rúanaid, who died in 665. The high king was king of all Ireland. Diarmaid Mac Murrough, the king of Leinster, brought the Anglo-Normans to Ireland for the first time. He asked them to help him against his enemies.

## Derry

*Descendant of the red-haired one*

A name that comes from the surname O Doireidh, meaning 'descendant of the red-haired one', and increasingly used today as a first name. It is also used as a pet form of Dermot.

# Desmond

A popular name in the English-speaking world derived from *Desmumhnach* ('man from Desmond'). Desmond was a province in Co. Cork; its name is derived from *Deas Mumhan* ('south Munster'). The province was the territory of several powerful dynasties: initially the MacCarthys, then the FitzGeralds, the Norman settlers.

*Dylan*
# Dillon
*Flash of lightning* or *faithful, loyal*
*Dylan*

This popular name is the Irish form of the Welsh name Dylan and is also a common surname. It has two possible derivations: it may come from the Irish word *dealan* ('flash of lightning') or from a word meaning 'faithful', 'loyal'.

*Donncha, Donnchadh, Donnchad*
# Donagh
*Brown-haired warrior*

This was the name of Brian Boru's eldest son, who became king of Munster when his father was killed at the Battle of Clontarf in 1014. He ruled from 1014 to 1064 and died in Rome. The name comes from *donnchadh*, which means 'brown-haired warrior'.

## Dónal

*Domhnall, Domnall*   **Dónal**   *Daniel; Donald*
*World-mighty*   *(in Scotland)*

One of the most ancient and popular Irish names, used throughout the country. Five high kings bore the name, including Domnall Ilchelgach ('of the many treacheries'), who died in 566. In the seventeenth century, Domnall was used as a generic name for an Irish Catholic. In mythology, Domhnall was a Scot who taught Cúchulainn the art of war. The names of the O'Donnell clan from Donegal and the MacDonnells of Antrim and Galloway are derived from this name. One of the few saints with this name is St Domnall. His feast day: 26 April.

## Duane

*Dwayne, Dwane*   **Duane**
*Descendant of the dark (-haired) one*

A surname now being used as a first name. It comes from O Dubain, meaning 'descendant of the dark (-haired) one'. The name was popularised by the rock guitarist Duane Eddy in the late 1950s and early 1960s and is very popular today in the Caribbean.

## Dubhlainn

**Dubhlainn**   *Doolin*
*Black sword*

A name derived from the combination of the Gaelic words *dubh* ('black') and *lan* ('blade', 'sword'). Dubhlainn loved the fairy queen and legendary harpist Aoibhell. A prophecy said he was to die in battle, but Aoibhell loved him so much she wove him a cloak that made him invisible.

## Dwyer

**Dwyer**
*Dark wisdom*

A popular first name, this is an anglicised form of the Irish surname O Duibhidir, which is made up of two elements: *dubh* ('black', 'dark') and *eidir* ('sense', 'wisdom').

| *Éamonn, Éamann* | # Éamon<br>*Rich protection* | *Edmund, Edward* |
|---|---|---|

The Irish form of Edmond or Edmund, the name was introduced into Ireland by the Anglo-Normans. It was the name of a ninth-century king and saint, martyred in 870, who gave his name to the English town of Bury St Edmunds. One of the most illustrious bearers of the name was Éamon de Valera, one of the great figures in Irish history. He fought in the 1916 Easter Rising, had a central role in the formation of the Republic of Ireland and was Ireland's president from 1959 to 1973. He died in 1975.

| *Aogán* | # Egan<br>*Little flame* |
|---|---|

This is the pet form of Aidan, and is also popular in Ireland as a surname, in this form and as Hagan and O'Hagan. It was the name of a great Irish poet, Aogán Ó Raithaille (1675–1729).

| *Eiméid* | # Emmet |
|---|---|

Originally a surname and now popular as a first name, it is a tribute to Robert Emmet (1778–1803), who led an unsuccessful rebellion of the United Irishmen against the British in 1798. His love for Sarah Curran led to his capture after an abortive Dublin uprising in 1803. He gave a moving speech from the dock at the scene of his execution in Dublin that same year, which began, 'When my country takes her place among the nations of the earth, then, and not till then, let my epitaph be written.'

## Enda
*Éanna, Énnae*
*Birdlike*

This was the name of several legendary Irish heroes, including Énnae Airgthech, a king of Munster. It was said he gave his warriors silver shields. The most famous bearer of the name is Énnae of Aran, the Irish monk. Born in Co. Meath, where his father was a chieftain, he was persuaded by his sister, St Fainche, to become a monk. He trained in Galloway in Scotland, and returned to Ireland to establish a monastery on Inishmore, the largest of the Aran islands, off the west coast. He died there *c*.530. His feast day: 21 March.

## Ennis
*Island* or *sole choice*

This name may be derived directly from the Irish word *inis* ('island') or taken from the place name Ennis, a town in Co. Clare that sits on an island between two streams of the River Fergus. Another possibility is that it means 'sole choice'.

## Eoghan
*Éogan*
*Born of the yew*
*Eugene, Owen*

A name that often appears in Irish mythology. Eoghan, the son of Durthacht, killed the sons of Usna, an Ulster chieftain, and was driving the chariot from which Deirdre threw herself. Eoghan was also the name of the son of Niall of the Nine Hostages. St Eoghan of Ardstraw, Co. Tyrone, was captured by pirates and taken to Britain. He escaped, studied in Galloway in Scotland and returned to Ireland to found a monastery at Ardstraw. He is the patron saint of Londonderry. His feast day: 23 August.

# Eoin

*John*

A very popular name used in Ireland since the earliest days of Christianity. It is the earliest Irish equivalent of John the apostle's name and came from the Latin Johannes. The later Irish form is Séan, which comes from French, and came into Ireland with the Anglo-Normans. One of the most famous Irishmen bearing the name was Eoin MacNeill. He was a founder of the Gaelic League, chief of staff of the Irish Volunteers, but opposed military action in the 1916 Easter Rising. He became Minister of Education in the first government of the Irish Free State. He was also a scholar, writing on Irish history and Celtic Ireland.

# Farrell

*Ferrel, Ferrell*

*Man of strength*

An anglicisation of the Irish name Fergal ('man of strength'), this name is widely used as a surname. In the United States, however, it is increasingly seen as a first name.

# Ferdia

*Ferdiad*

*Man of God*

A name probably derived from *fear* and *Dia* ('man of God'). Ferdia, from Connacht, was a friend of the great Ulster warrior Cúchulainn. When Queen Maeve of Connacht went to war with Ulster, Ferdia had to fight Cúchulainn because the latter was guarding a ford between the two provinces. The duel lasted for three days, and each night the friends tended each other's wounds. Cúchulainn only finally overcame his friend by letting loose his magical spear, the Gae Bolga, which killed Ferdia.

# Fergal
*Fearghal*

*Man of strength*

A name connected with the word *fear* ('man'), it has been popular in Ireland for centuries. It is also the source of the Irish surname Farrell. It is said to be the Irish name of St Virgilius, the non-ordained bishop of Salzburg, who died in 784. Fergal mac Máele Dúin became king of Ireland in 709. He was responsible for murders, for extracting tribute and demanding hostages, and was himself killed at the Hill of Allen in 722.

# Fergus
*Fearghus*

*Strength of a man*

An ancient Irish name, and one borne by at least ten saints. Fergus mac Róich was an Irish king and an important figure in the great Ulster saga *Táin Bó Cuailgne*. He was tricked out of the kingship of Ulster in favour of Conchobhar and eventually went into exile in Connacht. He was defeated in the ensuing battle against Ulster. In the sixth century, Fergus mac Erc led an army of Irishmen, known as Scoti, to colonise Argyll, thus giving Scotland its modern name.

# Fiachra
*Raven*

In mythology, this was the name of one of the three children of the sea god Lir, who was changed into a swan by his jealous stepmother, Aoife. St Fiachra, who came from Bangor, was the patron saint of travellers, and also of gardeners, because of the fine vegetables he grew around his hermitage at Meaux in France, where he died in 670. He also gave his name to a Parisian horse-drawn cab introduced in the seventeenth century. His feast day: 8 February. Fiacre is the French form of the name.

# Finbarr
*Finnbarr, Fionnbharr*
*Fair-haired*
*Barry*

A popular name in Ireland today and the name of one of the Tuatha Dé Danann ('people of Dana'), the mythical race said to have inhabited Ireland in the earliest times. They became the underground 'fairy people', and the superstitious still regard their 'fairy mounds' with respect. Several Irish saints have the name, but the most important is the seventh-century patron saint of Cork, who is said to have performed several miraculous cures. He founded a hermitage at Gúgáin Barra (Barra's Creek), near the source of the River Lee. However, he was told by angels to follow the river to the position of the present city, where he founded a monastery. His feast day: 25 September. Barre and Bairre are Irish 'pet' forms of the name; the latter is anglicised as Barry.

# Finn
*Fionn*
*Fair, light-hued*

The name of the most important Irish mythological hero, Fionn mac Cumhail, founder and leader of the Fianna, a warrior band of about 150 chieftains and 4,000 warriors, musicians, poets, priests and physicians. He acquired the gift of wisdom by touching the Salmon of Knowledge and sucking his thumb when he burnt it cooking the fish. He was Oisín's father and pursued Diarmaid and Gráinne. Twentieth-century Irish writers, such as James Joyce and Flann O'Brien, have used him in their work as an inspirational figure. In the United States, Finn is becoming a popular name for girls too.

# Finnegan
*Fionnagán*

A popular diminutive form of Finn.

## Finnian
*Finian, Finnén*

A name derived from the Irish name Finn, with an added British connection: St Finnian of Clonard, Co. Meath, and St Finnian of Movill, Co. Down, both spent time in Britain. It has been suggested that the name might be an early British form of Finbarr.

## Fintan
*Fionntán*
*White ancient or white fire*

The name of the Salmon of Knowledge, from which Fionn mac Cumhail derived his wisdom, and also the name of one of the sons of Niall of the Nine Hostages. Over 20 saints bear the name, of whom the best-known is St Fintan of Cloneenagh, Co. Laois: he founded a monastery there and is said to have lived on stale barley bread and muddy water. He had a reputation for recruiting disciples in an unorthodox way: it is said he persuaded a man with a wife, 12 sons and seven daughters 'to abandon this world's pleasures and assume the religious habit'. He died in 603. His feast day: 17 February.

## Flann
*Blood-red*

A very popular early name used by kings, queens, poets and saints. Semi-mythological character Flann mac Dima was the lover of the wife of sixth-century high king Diarmaid. The king set fire to a house to try to catch him and Flann drowned in a water tank while trying to escape. Another namesake was Flann Sinna, a high king of Tara, Co. Meath, who died in 916 after reigning 'for 36 years, six months and five days'. He is commemorated on one of the high crosses at Clonmacnoise, Co. Offaly. The name was popularised by the twentieth-century Irish writer Brian O'Nolan, who was known by his pen name, Flann O'Brien.

# Flynn
### Blood-red

Another example of a surname now used as a first name, it is derived from *flann* ('blood-red').

# Gael

According to legend, Gael was the ancestor of the Gaelic people. The name is probably derived from *gaedheal* ('Irish').

*Gearóid, Garalt, Gearalt*　　　# Garret
### Hard as a spear
　　　　　　*Gerald, Gerard*

A name with Germanic origins, introduced by the Anglo-Normans. With the prefix 'Fitz', FitzGerald became the surname of the most powerful Norman-Irish family in late medieval Ireland. Gearóid FitzGerald, the third Earl of Desmond (1338–98) was reputed to have magical powers (it was said he was the product of the rape by his father, Muirís, of the love goddess Áine). He was said to be 'a nobleman of wonderful bounty, cheerfulness in conversation, easy of access, charitable in deeds, a witty and ingenious composer of Irish music' and also wrote courtly love poetry. One tradition says he is not dead, but sleeping in Lough Gur, near his Co. Limerick castle, and will rise up when Ireland is in danger.

## Garvin
*Garbhán, Garbán, Garvan*
### *Rough*

The name of five early Irish saints. Little is known about them, but St Garbhán (of Kinsale, Co. Cork or Kinsealy, Co. Dublin), has his feast day on 9 July. It was also the name of an early king of Munster. Like many Irish first names, it can also be used as a surname.

## Glendon
*Glendan*
### *One from the fortress in the valley*

A name that comes from the Gaelic *gleann* (valley) and *dún* (fortress) that together give a meaning of 'one from the fortress in the valley'.

## Glenn
*Glen*
### *Valley*

From the Irish word *gleann* (valley), it is becoming popular as a first name, but is also used as a surname. The Hollywood star Glenn Ford popularised the name in the 1950s. The Welsh form, Glyn, has long been popular.

# Iarlaith

*Iarlaithe*                                          *Jarlath*

The name of the patron saint of Tuam, Co. Galway, who was ordained in 468 and known for his piety and constant prayer. He established his first monastery and school just west of Tuam, at Cloonfush. Two of his pupils were St Brendan of Clonfert and St Colman of Cloyne. He asked St Brendan to show him a good place to end his days. Brendan took him in a chariot but the wheels broke at Tuam. He founded a second monastery there and died there. His remains are buried on the site of the monastery.

# Iollan
*One who worships a different god*

Iollan was the son of the high king Fergus mac Roth and a champion at the court of Conchobhar mac Nessa. When Deirdre, who was betrothed to King Conchobhar, eloped to Scotland with Naoise, Iollan went with his father to persuade them to come back. He did so, but died defending them when it became clear that Conchobhar's motive had been revenge.

# Irial

An unusual and very old Irish name whose origin and meaning are obscure. It was revived by several families in the Middle Ages. Its attractive sound gives it a contemporary appeal.

## Kelly

*Ceallach*

*Bright-headed*

A name originally used for girls and boys, it is again finding favour for boys. Traditionally, it was thought to mean 'frequenter of churches', but opinion now holds that it is a much older name meaning 'bright-headed'. Since the mid-twentieth century it has become very popular in Britain, the United States, Canada and Australia as a girl's name again. It is also a very common Irish surname.

## Kennedy

*Cinnéide, Cennétig*

*Rough-headed* or *helmet-headed*

Cennétig mac Lorcain was the father of Brian Boru, Ireland's most famous king, who defeated the Vikings at the Battle of Clontarf in 1014. He united the warring dynasties in Ireland and broke the Viking hold on the country, but died in the battle. In mythology, Brian was the eldest of Tureann's three sons, the Celtic equivalents of the Greek Argonauts. Usually a surname, most famously of America's best-known political dynasty, Kennedy is now increasingly popular as a first name for both boys and girls.

## Kevin

*Caoimhín, Caoimhghin, Cáemgen*

*Beautiful birth* or *comely child*

The name of a seventh-century abbot, famous for his piety and patience. When he was a young celibate monk he hid in a bed of nettles to escape the attentions of a young woman. The monastery he established at Glendalough, Co. Wicklow, became an important site of pilgrimage, at one stage considered the equivalent of a pilgrimage to Rome. It is said that a blackbird flew on to his hand and laid her egg on it while he was praying one day. He remained kneeling until the egg was hatched and the bird flew away. He died *c*.620. Feast day: 3 June.

## Labhrás

*Labhras, Lubhrás*　　　　　*Laurel*　　　　　*Laurence*

Several Irish saints had this name, but the best-known was martyred in the third century. Within living memory in Ireland, people associated their suffering with his by saying: 'Labhrás, burned on a gridiron, pray for us.'

## Lee

*Leigh*　　　　　*Poem*

This is a popular name for both boys and girls. It may come from the Gaelic word *laoi* ('poem') or be a reference to the River Lee in Ireland.

## Lennán

*Leannán*　　　　　*Lover, sweetheart*　　　　　*Lennon*

A name that was very popular among the dynastic families of Co. Clare, the Corcu Baiscinn. One of their kings, Lennán mac Cathrannach, ruled from 898 to 915. The modern surname Lennon, for ever associated with John Lennon of the Beatles, who was murdered in 1980, is derived from this name. Because of that association, the name Lennon is now seen as a first name.

## Liam

A very popular name that was originally Uilliam, the Irish form of William. It was brought to England at the time of the Norman Conquest, and from there to Ireland. The name William had Germanic origins and was made up of elements meaning 'will' and 'helmet'.

## Lochlan

*Lochlann, Lochlainn*

*Viking*

*Laughlin*

This is the Irish form of a name that meant 'Viking' or 'Scandinavian', since Norway was known as Lochlainn, 'the land of the lochs'. It described the ninth- and tenth-century Viking and merchant invaders. It was given to boys with red or fair hair, and became a common surname in the north-west of Ireland.

## Lomán

*Lommán*

*Bare*

A name taken from the Irish word *lomm* ('bare'). St Lommán, the patron saint of Trim, Co. Meath, is the best-known of the saints with this name. Ancient tradition has it that Fedelmid, the lord of that district, presented 'his territory with all his goods and all of his race' to Lommán and St Patrick. The latter came to Ireland during his reign. Lommán, said to be Patrick's nephew, was the first bishop of the church Patrick founded at Trim and for generations his successors were chosen from Fedelmid's descendants. His feast day: 11 October.

## Lonán

*Blackbird*

A name derived from the word *lon* ('blackbird'). Several saints have the name, including St Lonán Finn (feast day: 22 January) and St Lonán of Trevet, Co. Meath (feast day: 1 November).

# Lorcán

*Lorccán*

*Fierce*

A very common name in early medieval Ireland and that of several kings. It is now growing in popularity. One of the best-known bearers of the name was the saint Lorcán Ó Tuathail (anglicised as Laurence O'Toole). He studied at the monastery at Glendalough, Co. Wicklow, becoming abbot there in 1153, and became archbishop of Dublin in 1162. He resisted the Anglo-Norman conquest of Ireland, but eventually submitted to the authority of Henry II of England. He died in 1180 in France, and was canonised by Pope Honorius III in 1226.
His feast day: 14 November.

*Martán*

# Máirtín
*Belonging to Mars*

*Martin*

Mars was the Roman god of war and the Irish form of the name was derived from the Latin for his name. It became popular in Ireland because of St Martin of Tours, a fourth-century soldier. It was also the name of the abbot of both Clonmacnoise, Co. Offaly, and Devenish, Co. Roscommon, who died in 868, and the bishop of Roscommon, who died in 915.

*Maoilseachlainn,*
*Maeleachlainn,*
*Malachi*

# Malachy
*My messenger*

Originally derived from an old Irish name meaning 'follower of St Sechnall', the name was given to high kings in the ninth and tenth centuries. The modern form became popular in the late Middle Ages and comes from the name of the Old Testament prophet Malachi. It became popular in Ireland because of two saints. The first was the archbishop of Armagh, Maolmaodhog (1094–1148), a papal legate, who reformed the Church in Ireland and brought it closer to Rome and Europe. He was canonised by Pope Clement III in 1190. His feast day: 3 November. The second saint is St Sechnall, one of St Patrick's first converts.

*Mánus, Maghnus*

# Manus
*Great*

A name popular in the north-west of Ireland. It was adopted by the Norsemen in honour of the Holy Roman Emperor, Carolus Magnus (742–814), known as Charlemagne, and introduced by them into Ireland. Charlemagne's court in Aachen was a centre of learning and art; his teachers came mainly from Ireland.

## Meallán
*Mellán*
*Lightning*

The name of several Irish saints, among them one who was with a group of Irish clerical students said to have met St Patrick. The saint blessed them and gave them a skin to hold their books. The student went on to found a church at Kilrush, Co. Westmeath, and became a bishop, which St Patrick had predicted. His feast day: 28 January.

## Mel

The origins of this name are not known but St Mel, the bishop and patron saint of Ardagh, Co. Limerick (died 487; feast day: 6 February), is its most famous bearer. He was St Patrick's nephew and established a monastery at Ardagh. He was reputed – wrongly – to have had a relationship with one of Patrick's sisters, Lupita, who was staying in the monastery. As a result, Patrick issued a decree that 'consecrated men and women – even though nearly related – should live apart, and in separate habitations, lest the weak might be scandalised, or that any injury might be inflicted on religious decorum, by the existence of possible causes leading to temptation.'

## Mícheál
*Míchél*
*Who is like the Lord*
*Michael*

This name is taken from one of the biblical Archangels and, like many Irish names, given a Gaelic equivalent. In the nineteenth and twentieth centuries it was very common. One of the most famous modern bearers of the name was the Irish writer and actor Mícheál Mac Liammóir (1899–1978). In 1928 he and Hilton Edwards launched the famous Gate Theatre in Dublin. It brought plays by major European writers to Ireland and provided a platform for plays by Irish writers.

# Milo

The Irish names Maeleachlainn, Maolmhuire and Maolmordha, all beginning with *mael/maol* ('devotee of…') were anglicised as Myles and Miles. Milo is an Irish form of these names.

# Muiris
### *Dark-skinned, Moorish*     *Maurice*

This is the Irish form of the name Maurice, introduced into Ireland by the Anglo-Normans and taken from the Latin Mauricius. It was popular because of St Maurice, the Christian captain of a Theban legion, martyred with all his men in Switzerland in the third century by order of Maximinian for refusing to take part in heathen sacrifice.

# Murphy
### *Hound of the sea*

Murphy was originally a nickname, then a first name, and later a well-known Irish surname. It is now becoming popular again as a first name for both boys and girls in the United States. It is derived from the Irish word *murchú* ('hound of the sea').

# Murtagh
*Murchadh*     ### *Skilled in seacraft, sea battler*     *Murdoch (in Scotland)*

This was the name of three high kings of Ireland and one of Ireland's greatest military commanders, Murtagh of the Leather Cloak. In midwinter 926, wearing leather cloaks to keep warm, he beat the Vikings in a sea battle on Strangford Lough. He captured and burned Viking Dublin in 939, attacked the Norse settlements in the Scottish islands with an Ulster fleet in 941 and died in combat in 943.

# Naoise

*Nyce* or *Noah*

This name has become popular as a result of the revival of interest in Celtic mythology. In legend, Naoise was the eldest of the three sons of Usna, an Ulster chieftain. Naoise was the lover of Deirdre, who was betrothed to the king of Ulster, Conchobhar mac Nessa. Deirdre said Naoise was exactly the man she wanted, with 'hair the colour of a raven's wing, cheeks the colour of fresh blood, and skin as white as snow'. He fled with her and his brothers to Scotland to escape the king. They were persuaded to return, but all three brothers were treacherously murdered. The name may be associated with the word *nasc* ('bond').

# Nevan

*Naomhán*

Saint, holy one

A name derived from the Irish word *naomb* ('saint', 'holy one') and so originally a nickname for a churchman or a religious person. It was also the name of an Irish saint (feast day: 13 September). It was then used as a first name and later a surname.

# Niall

*Champion* or *passionate, vehement*

*Neil, Neill, Neal*

An ancient name of uncertain derivation, but increasingly popular. Niall of the Nine Hostages was the semi-mythological king of Tara, in Co. Meath, so the name was given to Irish kings and clan chieftains. It has been suggested that Niall either took hostages from those he defeated in battle or that neighbouring clans gave him a hostage to prove their peaceful intentions. Sithchenn, the smith who lived in Tara, made sure Niall was chosen over his four brothers to succeed his father as king. He lured all the brothers into his forge and set fire to it. Niall brought out the anvil. The surnames MacNeill and O'Neill also come from the name.

## Nollaig
### Christmas

*Noel*

This is the Irish word for Christmas, taken from the French form Noël. It has only become popular as a first name in modern times, and can be given to a boy or girl, most often those born on 25 December.

## Nuada
### Newly made

Nuada was a king of the gods of ancient Ireland, the Tuatha Dé Danann, who lost his hand in battle. Diancecht, the physician of the gods, made him a silver hand so perfect he could pick up a pinch of salt with it. Diancecht's son, Miach, transplanted a hand of flesh and blood on to Nuada's arm.

## Nuadha
### Cloud-maker

*Nuadu*

An ancient name associated with a god, possibly the lord of the Otherworld or the god of fishermen. In very early writings, Nuadu is a legendary hero and the ancestor of many noble families: Nuadu Necht, for example, is said to be the legendary ancestor of the Leinstermen. Despite its pagan origins, the name was given to heroes, saints and clerics, including St Nuadu the anchorite (hermit) (feast day: 3 October); and St Nuadu of Clones (feast day: 1 December). It was also the name of the abbot of Tuam and the abbot of Armagh, in the eighth and ninth centuries respectively.

## Odhrán

*Odrán, Órán, Orin*　　　　*Dun-coloured, sallow*　　　　*Oran*

The name of several saints, the most important of whom was St Patrick's charioteer. St Patrick was on a mission in Munster and a chieftain, Failge Berraide, decided to assassinate him. Odhrán heard of the plot and, pretending to be tired, persuaded St Patrick to change places with him and drive the chariot himself. When they were ambushed, Odhrán was killed. St Oran, the abbot of Meath, was one of 12 people who went with St Columba to the island of Iona to spread Christianity in Scotland: there is a St Oran's well on the island.

## Oilibhéar

*Oileabhéar*　　　　*Relic of God or olive tree*　　　　*Oliver*

A name derived either from the Norse Olaf ('relic of God') or from the Latin word for 'olive tree', so meaning peace and safety. It was introduced into Ireland by the Anglo-Normans, but became very unpopular in the seventeenth century because of its association with Oliver Cromwell, the scourge of Ireland. It returned to favour because of a saint, Archbishop Oliver Plunkett (1625–81), who was executed at Tyburn in London for treason and canonised in 1976. His head was preserved and kept as a relic in Drogheda, one of the towns where Cromwell carried out an atrocity.

## Oisín

*Oissíne*

*Little deer*

*Ossian*

An old name that is very popular again. Oisín was the son of Fionn mac Cumhail, the most important of Ireland's mythological heroes, who founded and led the Fianna, a band of chieftains, warriors, musicians, poets, priests and physicians. Oisín was the poet of the Fianna and a warrior. It is said that his goddess mother Sive reared him in the forest because she had been turned into a doe. Fionn found him and claimed him as his son. Oisín was also the lover of Niamh, with whom he spent 300 years in Tír-na-n-Óg (the Land of Eternal Youth). It is also the name of four Irish saints.

## Oscar

*Osgar*

*Deer lover*

In legend, Oscar was the son of Oisín, the great warrior of the Fianna, and so the grandson of Fionn mac Cumhail. In time, Oscar himself became the most celebrated warrior of his day. The Irish writer Oscar Wilde (1854–1900) was the most famous bearer of the name, which fell from favour after the scandal surrounding Wilde's trial. It is now regaining popularity, and has always been used in America. Napoleon Bonaparte, the emperor of France, was so impressed by a poem about Oscar, written by the Scottish poet James Macpherson, that he gave his grandson the name: the child became Oscar I of Sweden.

# Patrick
*Pádraig, Pádraic, Pátraic*
### Noble

The name of Ireland's national saint and the quintessential Irish name. It has, however, been popular as a first name for less than 300 years. St Patrick was so revered that his name was not given to children for hundreds of years after his death, except in the form Gilla Pátraic ('servant of Patrick'). There are many legends and traditions about St Patrick (feast day: 17 March), but he was probably born in Britain, captured as a youth by Irish raiders, escaped and trained as a priest in Europe. He made his way back to Ireland and established Christianity as the country's national religion. From 432, he established churches throughout Ireland, over 60 with bishops, the majority of whom were Irishmen consecrated by him. He is said to have performed many miracles and fasted for 40 days on Croagh Patrick, in Co. Mayo. He died in 463. The name Patrick was popular among the Anglo-Normans before it was used by the Irish, who found Irish forms.

# Peadar
*Peadair*　　　　　　　　　　　　　　　　　　*Peter*
### Rock

The Irish form of Peter, the name of the chief apostle of Christ. The name continues to be very popular because of its provenance. Peadar is a comparatively recent form. Originally the form Piaras was used, which came from Piers, introduced into Ireland by the Normans.

## Pearse

*Piaras*                                          *Pearce, Pierce, Piers*

This name is also a form of Peter (Piaras was taken from the Norman Piers), and was so popular that it was also adopted as a surname. This is the case with Patrick J. Pearse (1879–1916), the leader of the 1916 Easter Rising in Dublin. The connection with him is one of the main reasons for the name's continuing popularity in Ireland.

## Phelan
### Wolf

*Faolán, Felan*

A name taken from a literary word, *faol* ('wolf'). The earliest record of its use appears to be for a follower of the legendary warrior Fionn mac Cumhail. He was so loyal that nothing on earth or in heaven could keep him from his lord.

## Phelim
### Constant

*Feidhlim, Feidhlimid, Felim*

An ancient name that occurs in legend and in early royal records: three kings of Munster bore the name. Warriors and poets have also been given the name. Felim was the father of Deirdre, who was the lover of Naoise and was betrothed to the king of Ulster, Conchobhar mac Nessa. It was also the name of Colum Cille's father, so it is most commonly found in Donegal.

# Piaras

*Perais, Ferus*

This name exists in its own right, borrowed from Piers, the Norman form of the biblical name Peter. Those of Norman descent were still using it in Ireland in the seventeenth century. Piaras Feiritéir fought on the side of the indigenous Irish in the rising of 1641, the last of the Kerry commanders to submit to Oliver Cromwell. He seized Tralee Castle, but was wounded in the attack. He was promised safe conduct but was hanged on Martyrs' Hill, Killarney, in 1653, with a priest and a bishop. He was also a scholar and poet, known for his courtly love poems.

# Pilib

*Filib*       *Lover of horses*       *Philip*

The Anglo-Normans brought this name to Ireland. It is the Irish form of Philip, which was itself taken from the Greek. It was the name of one of Christ's 12 apostles and is a very appropriate name for an Irish boy, since the Irish are born with a love of horses in their blood.

# Pól

*Póil*       *Little one*       *Paul*

The Irish version of Paul, which was taken from the Latin *paulus* ('small'). It is, of course, the name of the biblical St Paul, but only became popular in Ireland when Paul VI became Pope in 1963 (he died in 1978).

# Proinsias
*Proinnsias, Proinnséas,*        *Frenchman*        *Francis*
*Próinsias*

This name is an Irish form of Francis, taken from the Latin Franciscus ('Frenchman') and borrowed from St Francis of Assisi (1181–1226), the patron saint of birds and animals. It is said that St Francis was given the name when he was a young man because he learnt to speak French so readily. The name was popularised in Ireland by the Franciscan order of monks.

# Quinlan
*Quinlevan, Quinlivan,*        *Of beautiful shape*
*Quilan*

Another example of a contemporary surname now being used as a first name. It is probably derived from *caoindealbhán* ('of beautiful shape').

# Quinn
*Quin*        *Intelligent*

This name is probably a variant of the name Conn, meaning 'intelligent'. It is the most common surname in Co. Tyrone in Northern Ireland, and is now being used increasingly as a first name, particularly in the USA, for both boys and girls.

# Randal

*Raghnall, Ragnall,*
*Ranulf*

*Mighty power* or *ruler's advice*

A name that came from the Old Norse name Ragnvald ('ruler's advice') and was borne by many Vikings who settled in Ireland. It was popular by the eleventh century: Raghnall mac Amláib was a Norseman killed at the Battle of Tara, Co. Meath, in 980; Raghnall mac Ímair, the king of Waterford, died in 1018.

# Redmond

*Réamonn, Réamann,*
*Rémann*

*Protector, counsellor*

*Raymond*

The name is an Irish version of an old Germanic name made up of two elements, *rad* and *mund*, meaning 'counsellor' and 'protector'. It was a common Norman name and came to Ireland with Strongbow and his adventurers. It was particularly popular in Northern Ireland. Redmond O'Hanlon, a notorious seventeenth-century highwayman there, inspired the verse: 'Twixt Fivemiletown and Crossmaglen, there are more thieves than honest men.' His father's estate was confiscated by the English during the Cromwellian settlement and Redmond, his three brothers and about 50 followers became outlaws. They were known as the 'Rapparees', seeking vengeance on those who had taken Irish lands.

# Reilly

*Raghallaigh*

*Courageous, valiant*

*Riley*

Another example of an Irish surname that is now used as a first name, principally in the USA. It is related to the Gaelic word *rafaireacht* ('prosperity').

## Riordan
*Ríoghbhardán, Rearden*
*Royal poet*

A name derived from *ri* ('king') and *bardan* ('poet'), it was first used to describe the profession of royal poet, then became a first name and later a surname. It is now being used as a first name again, particularly in the USA and Canada. In an Irish royal household the poet was very highly esteemed, acting as scholar, historian and adviser to the king.

## Risteárd
*Strong ruler*
*Richard*

A variant of the name Riocárd, introduced into Ireland by the Normans. Risteárd is now the common form. The name was one of the most common among the Anglo-Norman settlers in Ireland. Its popularity is due to a seventh-century Anglo-Saxon king of Kent, who bore the name. He gave up his throne and became a monk in Lucca, Italy, where he was said to have performed many miracles.

## Ronan
*Rónán*
*Little seal*

From the Gaelic word *rón* ('seal'), this is an ancient Irish name. Celtic legend tells of a seal who is warned not to stray too close to land, but who is swept ashore by a huge wave and trapped in a human form, as a 'sea maiden'. She lives with a fisherman and their children are known as 'ronans' or 'little seals'. She never loses her longing for the sea, however. She finds her 'seal skin' hidden by her husband and slips back to the ocean, but cannot forget her family and can be seen swimming close to shore, keeping a watchful eye on them. Several saints bear the name. St Ronan Finn (died 664; feast day: 22 May) put a curse on his tormentor, Suibhne Gelt ('Mad' Sweeney), who subsequently lost his mind and spent the rest of his life wandering the woods of Ireland as a wild bird-man.

# Rory
*Ruaidhrí, Ruairí, Ruarí*
*Red king* or *great king*

A favourite name in medieval Ireland, and that of the last high king, Ruaidhrí Ua Conchobhar (died 1198), who made peace with Henry II of England. It was also the name of a famous sixteenth-century Irish sculptor, Ruaidhrí Ó Tunney, of the Kilkenny school, whose workshop was at nearby Callan.

# Rúadhán
*Rúadán*
*Little redhead* or *red-haired*
*Rowan*

This name has been associated with the rowan tree since the time of the Vikings. The rowan is sometimes associated with the tree on which Christ was crucified. In Gaelic mythology, the warrior Rúadhán is the son of Brigit and Bres. It is also the name of several saints, the most famous being St Rúadán, who founded the monastery at Lorrha, Co. Tipperary, in the sixth century (feast day: 15 April). One story says he saved a fugitive from the king by hiding him in his cellar. When the king asked where he was, the saint said, 'I don't know, unless he's under your feet.' Like many Irish saints, he also had the power to cure lepers. When a group arrived at the monastery, he stuck his staff into the ground, water gushed out, and when the lepers bathed in it they were cured.

# Ryan
*Rían, Ríoghán, Rígán*
*Little king*

The name of saints and warriors, it is mainly a surname in Ireland, but very popular in Britain, the United States and Australia as a first name. Two ninth-century bearers of the name were Rígán, the son of Fergus, who was killed in battle against Connacht in 845, and Rían, son of Bruddai, killed by the Vikings in 895. St Rían's feast day is 23 April.

# Seamus

*Séamas, Seumas, Seumus*　　*A supplanter* or *he who takes by the heel*　　*James*

A popular name, it is the Irish form of the biblical name James and was common among the Anglo-Norman settlers in Ireland. Notable twentieth-century bearers of the name are the Nobel poet laureate, Seamus Heaney, and Seamus Murphy, a famous Cork sculptor and stone-carver. He was born near Mallow in 1907 and created busts of many prominent people, among them all the Irish presidents. He died in Cork in 1975.

# Sean

*Séan, Seaghán, Séon*　　*God is gracious*　　*John; also Shaun and Shawn; Shane (in Northern Ireland)*

The Irish form of John, this was one of the commonest names among the early Anglo-Norman settlers in Ireland. Sean is a more recent variation of Eóin. In time Sean became the most popular boy's name in Ireland and was popularised outside the country by the actor Sean Connery. Séan Lemass (1899–1971) was born in Dublin and fought in the 1916 Easter Rising and on the Republican side in the Civil War. He was a founder-member of the political party Fianna Fáil and Minister for Industry in De Valera's first government in 1932. He served as Taoiseach (the prime minister of the Irish Republic) from 1959 to 1966. The phonetic spellings Shaun and Shawn are very popular in Britain and the United States, and Shane in Northern Ireland.

# Séathrún

*Séafraidh, Séafra, Séafraid*　　　　　　　　*Geoffrey*

The Irish form of Geoffrey, which was introduced into Ireland by the Anglo-Normans. Irish historian and poet Séathrún Ceitinn (*c.*1570–1650) was born in Co. Tipperary and trained as a priest in an Irish college in Bordeaux, France. He was famous for his sermons and for writing a history of Ireland. He toured the country doing research for the history.

## Senan

*Seanán, Sionán*

*Old, i.e. wise*

The most famous holder of this name was Seanán of Kilrush, who founded an important island monastery in the sixth century on Inis Cathaig, off the Co. Clare coast in the Shannon estuary. He is said to have got rid of a monster that inhabited the island and arranged with the angel accompanying him that there would always be safe passage for his monks to and from the island. Pebbles from the island are therefore believed to give protection from shipwreck. His feast day: 8 March. The name was first used as a respectful title, then developed into a first name.

## Seosamh

*Seosap, Seosaph*

*God shall add (another son)*

*Joseph*

This is now the usual Irish form of the biblical name Joseph. In pre-Norman times, however, the form for the name of the Virgin Mary's carpenter husband was Iósep. He was greatly respected by the early Celtic Church and later became the patron saint of workmen.

## Shanley

*Venerable warrior*

A name that is more usually seen as a surname, but is ripe for popularity as a first name because of its meaning. It is derived from the Irish *sean laoch*, which means 'venerable warrior'.

## Sorley
*Somhairle*
### Summer wanderer

An Ulster name that comes from Old Norse and is particularly popular with the MacDonnells of Antrim. In Ireland it became a generic word for Viking, because the Vikings sailed south to raid the coastlines of Ireland and Scotland during the summer, when the weather was better and the journey less hazardous. Somhairle Mac Donnell (1505–90), a thorn in the side of Queen Elizabeth I of England, was imprisoned in Dublin Castle from 1551 to 1552. When he was released, he seized the constable of Carrickfergus and demanded a ransom. He was defeated at Toome in 1575 by Essex. His wife and family, whom he had sent to Rathlin Island for safety, were killed by Sir John Norris, along with the whole of the island's population. Sir Francis Drake was the naval commander in the action.

## Suibhne
*Suibne*                                              *Sweeney*
### Well-going

The name of seven Irish saints, but the most famous character with this name was Suibhne Gelt ('Mad' Sweeney). Legend has it that he was a seventh-century king of Ireland. He was angered by the incessant ringing of St Ronan's church bells and threw the saint's prayerbook into a lake. St Ronan cursed him and Suibhne is said to have lost his wits. He went to live in the treetops with the birds and flew south in winter. Sweeney has become a contemporary surname.

# Tadhg
### Poet, philosopher

*Tadc*　　　　　　　　　　　　　　　　　*Timothy, Tad (USA)*

An ancient Irish name and that of several kings and princes, including Brian Boru's son, who died in 1023. St Tadhg was martyred at Wurtzburg (his feast day: 8 July). An anglicised form, Teague, was the standard stage name for an Irishman. In modern Irish, Tadhg is used to mean 'the man', as in 'the man in the street' or 'the man in the moon'.

# Tiernan
### Lord

*Tiarnán, Tighearnán, Tigernán*

This was a popular name in early Ireland, given to chieftains, kings and princes. It is usually associated with the surname O'Rourke: the twelfth-century warlike king of Breifne (Cavan, Leitrim and part of Longford) was Tiarnán O'Ruairc. He changed sides so often that by 1152 he had lost his fortress at Dangan and his territorial gains. He lost his wife, Dervorguilla, to Diarmaid Mac Murrough and was assassinated in 1172 by the Anglo-Normans. St Tiernan of Co. Mayo was an early saint (feast day: 8 April). Tiernan is also used as a surname.

# Tomás
### Twin

*Thomas*

The Irish form of the biblical name Thomas, one of Christ's disciples. The name was originally used only by the clergy: Tomás, abbot of Linn-Duachail, for example, died in 807. It became popular in Ireland as a first name via the Anglo-Normans, who were devoted to Thomas à Becket, Henry II's Archbishop of Canterbury, murdered in Canterbury Cathedral on the king's orders in 1170. A modern bearer of the name was the author Tomás Ó Criomhthain (1856–1937), who was born and died on Great Blasket island, off the Kerry coast. His book, *The Islandman*, described the hardship and isolation of island life, and was written, he said, because 'there will not be our likes again'.

# Torcán
*Wild boar*

A name derived from the Irish word *torcc* ('wild boar').

# Tuathal
*Leader or prince of the people*

*Tully*

An ancient name that was given to many Irish kings and heroes, though less common in modern times. It has also been used as a nickname and a surname, but its attractive Gaelic form and meaning suggest it is ripe for popularity again.

*Toirdhealbhach,*
*Tairdelbach,*
*Traolach*

# Turlough
*Instigator, abettor or shaped like*
*Thor (the Norse god of thunder)*

*Terence*

This name became very popular in the Middle Ages: several eleventh- and twelfth-century Irish kings had the name, including Tairdelbach úa Conchobhar, king of Connacht and high king of Ireland, who died in 1156. It was also the name of the famous blind harpist and composer, Turlough O'Carolan (1670–1732), who wrote in Irish Gaelic. He was blinded by smallpox at the age of 14.

# Tyrone

Taken from the name of the Irish county, Co. Tyrone, Tir Eoghan ('Land of Eoghan'). The name became popular in the twentieth century through Tyrone Guthrie, the theatre director, and the film actor Tyrone Power. Both men were related through a great-grandfather, who was born in Ireland, in Waterford.

## Uinseann
*Conquering*

*Uinsionn*                                                                                                    *Vincent*

The Irish form of Vincent, taken from the Latin Vincentius ('conquering'). The name was introduced into Ireland by the Anglo-Normans, but its popularity is mainly due to the fame of St Vincent de Paul, who founded orders all over the world to care for the poor and sick.

## Ultan
*Ulsterman*

*Ultán, Ultach*

This name was popular in the early period, with 18 saints of the name, including the most famous, St Ultán, the seventh-century abbot, bishop and scholar of Ardbraccan, Co. Meath, who is the patron saint of Ireland's children. He was known for austerity, bathing in cold water whatever the weather: another name for the Ardbraccan monastery was Ultan's Well. St Ultán is said to have 'fed with his own hands every child in Erin who had no support', particularly children of women who died of plague. His scholarly works included a poem and a life of St Brigid. His feast day: 4 September.

## Usna
*Temple of the head*

In legend, Usna was an Ulster chieftain, and the father of three sons, Naoise, Ainle and Ardan. Naoise fell in love with Deirdre, who was betrothed to the king of Ulster, Conchobhar mac Nessa. She and all three brothers fled, but when they returned to Ireland, all the brothers were treacherously killed by Conchobhar.